FROM EVE TO ESTHER

NELL W. MOHNEY

From Eve to Esther

Letting Old Testament Women Speak to Us

DIMENSIONS
FOR LIVING
NASHVILLE

FROM EVE TO ESTHER
LETTING OLD TESTAMENT WOMEN SPEAK TO US

This book is printed on acid-free, elemental-chlorine–free paper.

Library of Congress Cataloging in Publication Data [applied for]

ISBN 0-687-09622-7

01 02 03 04 05 06 07 08 09 10—10 9 8 7 6 5 4 3 2 1

MANUFACTURED IN THE UNITED STATES OF AMERICA

To my good friend and competent editor,

Sally Sharpe,

who truly seeks to perform her roles

as wife, mother, and career woman

through biblical principles

CONTENTS

ACKNOWLEDGMENTS

I express grateful appreciation to the following persons:

My husband and best friend, Ralph W. Mohney, Sr.,
for his indefatigable work at the computer,
an instrument that totally frustrates me,
and for his lighthearted encouragement when I grew weary
of the entire project.

The personnel of the Reference and Fine Arts Departments
of the Hamilton County Bicentennial Library,
for their willingness to do endless research at my request.

Mary Lee Sims, a voracious reader and a good friend,
who discovered excellent "rescue books" for me to read.

A young women's circle in my church, whose members allowed me
to try out some of the material on them.

INTRODUCTION

*T*he people of the Bible have enriched my life tremendously. Not only have they helped me understand the culture of Bible times, but they also have made the Bible "come alive" for me. More importantly, God has spoken clearly and graphically to me through many of these individuals.

The New Testament character of Barnabas, for example, opened my eyes to the importance of being an encourager. The disciples were apprehensive about accepting Paul as a true believer because he had been a persecutor of Christians. It was Barnabas who opened the door for Paul (Acts 9:27). When Barnabas was asked to lead the church in Antioch, he invited Paul to join him (Acts 11:22-25). The two of them took the first missionary journey together. Then, when Paul refused to take Mark on the second journey, Barnabas organized an alternate mission trip, which gave Mark—who had left the first journey because of homesickness and the rigors of the trip—a second chance at missionary work (Acts 15:36-40). As I read about Barnabas, I felt that God was calling me to be a cheerleader for others—to help them discover their leadership opportunities in the kingdom of God.

Even more explicitly, God has spoken to me through the women of the Bible—women with whom we have much in common, despite the fact that they lived in a time and culture vastly different from our own. Some of these women are little known while others are more widely familiar, yet they all have valuable lessons to offer. Hence came the idea for this book—and a second to follow on women of the New Testament.

As the title conveys, this book takes us from Eve, the prototype of the earliest woman, to Esther, who had the courage to take a risk for God. In between, we meet six interesting and dynamic women of the Old Testament, including Keturah, the second wife of Abraham, who has something to teach women living in blended families; Zipporah, the wife of Moses, who demonstrates how not to be a spouse; and Miriam, who was the original career woman. Because the Scriptures often tell us little about some of these women, I have used the work of biblical scholars, research findings about the customs of the day, and my own imagination to fill in the blank places. Each chapter begins with a retelling of a particular woman's story, followed by the practical and spiritual lessons that her story offers us. A Scripture text is provided so that you may read the biblical account for yourself. Every chapter ends with questions for reflection or discussion to help individuals or groups "dig a little deeper." Some chapters also include biblical affirmations "for the journey ahead."

As you read and use the material provided in this book, my hope is that you will listen carefully for God and open your heart, through prayerful listening, to receive the message God has for you. In his book *There's a Lot More to Health Than Not Being Sick* (Word, 1981), Dr. Bruce Larson tells of a conversation he had with noted Swiss psychiatrist Paul Tournier. Dr. Tournier, a strong Christian as well as a psychiatrist, said that he and his wife Nellie had their morning devotions together. Then they had separate periods of silence during which they concentrated on God's word from their devotional in a time of prayerful listening. Dr. Tournier said that as he did this, he regularly received messages about his treatment of patients, his relationship with his wife or other significant persons, and the specific concerns he faced.

In prayerful silence, God, through the Holy Spirit, can get through to our cluttered and distracted minds. Two scriptures remind me of this: "In quietness and in confidence shall be your strength" (Isaiah 30:15, KJV); and "They that wait upon the

LORD shall renew their strength; they shall mount up with wings as eagles; they shall run, and not be weary; and they shall walk, and not faint" (Isaiah 40:31, KJV). May you hear God speaking to circumstances in your own life through these women of the Old Testament.

1.

Eve

Learning to Handle Temptation

Scripture Text: **Genesis 3:1-24**

The man said, "The woman whom you gave to be with me, she gave me fruit from the tree, and I ate." Then the LORD God said to the woman, "What is this that you have done?" The woman said, "The serpent tricked me, and I ate."

—Genesis 3:12-13

Eve's Story

It was midmorning in the garden of Eden. The sun was shining brightly through the clear, unpolluted air. Everywhere there was beauty—lush, green vegetation; tall, stately trees; flowers of every color blooming in abundance; and fruits and vegetables for the taking. All these were gifts from God to allow his newly created human beings to live harmoniously and joyfully while staying in daily communication with their Creator.

Eve was enjoying the beauty of the garden while she picked some fruits and vegetables for their noon meal. Suddenly, the Tempter, in the form of a snake, slithered up beside her. He seemed perfectly harmless—indeed, a pleasant and interesting conversationalist—when he suggested that she pick the luscious fruit from the tree in the center of the garden.

"I can't do that," said Eve, as she bit into the sweetness of a tree-ripened peach.

"Why not?" asked the Tempter.

"God told us that we don't need the fruit from that tree. It is the tree of the knowledge of good and evil, and God alone knows how to distinguish between good and evil. If we trust and follow God, God will show us that distinction."

In a beguiling voice, the Tempter asked, "Did God tell you not to eat any fruit in the garden?"

"Oh, no!" replied Eve, as she finished her peach. "We can eat from every tree except the one in the center. If we eat from that tree, we will surely die."

The Tempter laughed uproariously and replied, "Oh, you won't die. But God knows that when you eat of that tree, your eyes will be opened, and you will be like God. You will know good from evil."

Hmm. Like God? thought Eve. It was a new and very appealing thought. She began to look at the tree in a new way. The thought of eating that fruit had never occurred to her before. Suddenly, she hungered for the forbidden fruit. The Tempter didn't need to say more. His temptation had found fertile ground.

Only later would Eve realize that God had not created her and Adam as puppets. They were given free choice. They could use it however they chose, but they couldn't control the consequences. God, in his love, had given them instructions not to inhibit them, but to allow them to continue to experience the peace and joy they had been given.

It wasn't long before Eve walked over to the tree, chose a ripe fruit, and found that it was delicious. Almost immediately, she knew she had done wrong; but she didn't want to be alone in her guilt. She ran to their home under the shade of two mighty oak trees, where

Adam was arranging leaves for a more comfortable bed. As she smiled sweetly and batted her eyelashes, she said, "Adam, this is the most delicious fruit I've ever tasted. Here, have a bite."

Looking up from his task, Adam asked in surprise, "Isn't that from the tree in the center of the garden? We are not supposed to eat . . ."

"Oh, the serpent told me that was a myth. We won't die. We will just get wiser. In fact, we will be like gods."

Adam looked at his beautiful wife. She certainly didn't look like a person who was about to die. In fact, she seemed to be enjoying the fruit. So Adam reached for the fruit—a fatal mistake! Adam began to understand that God didn't mean physical death but spiritual death—separation from God.

Both Adam and Eve became aware of their nakedness. They felt guilty and vulnerable, and they hid from God. Suddenly, they each became like two persons inside—one was loving and eager for communion with God; the other was dark and rebellious, full of pride and wanting to control. Their internal civil war had begun. Years later, Edward Sandford Martin would describe their predicament—and ours—in his poem that describes the tensions and strivings within each of us. He ends with these lines:

> From much corroding care I should be free
> If I could once determine which is me.

That evening, when it came time for their nightly conversation with God, Adam and Eve didn't walk toward God in anticipatory joy. In fact, God had to call them several times. Adam replied that they had realized they were naked and had sewn fig leaves together for aprons, but that they still were afraid to stand before God. God asked if they had eaten of the fruit of the forbidden tree. Their replies resound to this day. Adam said: "The woman whom you gave to be with me, she gave me fruit from the tree, and I ate"; and Eve said, "The serpent tricked me, and I ate" (Genesis 3:12-13). The blame game had begun—and has continued throughout all these centuries!

Before God sent Adam and Eve out of the garden into the hardships of the world (*East of Eden*, as John Steinbeck called it in his novel by the same name), he gave them clothes to wear. Later, through the prophet Isaiah, God promised that One would come who would bring reconciliation. The coming One would one day crush the head of the serpent—evil—who had had the conversation with Eve (Genesis 3:15). As Adam and Eve walked into a world that would be strange and hard and full of uncertainty, God sent them out with hope. God would send One to be the Reconciler and Redeemer.

The promised Redeemer did come, and his name is Jesus. God provided a way for us to return to oneness with our Creator. The dual nature of Adam and Eve is still in us, but unification and harmony are offered to all who accept this gift of grace through Jesus the Christ.

What Can We Learn From Eve?

Lesson 1: We must learn to attack temptation at first thought.

Temptation can come to us in subtle and beguiling ways. Perhaps, at first, we are repulsed by it. Next we begin to entertain the thought of the act. Then we tolerate and rationalize the act. Finally, we embrace it. Often it happens so subtly that we hardly are aware of it, which is why we must learn to recognize and attack it at first thought.

I have heard of an interesting laboratory experiment with frogs. If you put frogs into boiling water, they will jump out immediately; if you put them into cold water, then heat the water slowly, they won't be aware of the danger. Eventually, they are cooked in the boiling water. Often we are like those frogs. The promise of "playing God" by making our own choices and doing as we please appeals to our pride. The idea of "being in control" is powerful. We do not always realize the danger of yielding to temptation until it's too late!

Let me be clear: I do believe that God wants us to have courage, confidence, and pride—not in ourselves, but in our Christian heritage; not because of what we have accomplished, but because of whose we are. We all are made in the image of God (Genesis 1:27), and we all have broken the image (Romans 3:23). Yet we have been redeemed by Christ (John 3:16); and if we choose to accept our redemption, we are empowered to live victoriously in the here and now through the power of the Holy Spirit who comes to live within us (John 14:16-17). You see, it is the Holy Spirit that enables us to resist temptation. This doesn't mean we are not tempted. We all are tempted, even as Jesus himself was tempted (Matthew 4:1-11). But when we yield to the Holy Spirit living within us, we are given the supernatural ability *not to yield* to temptation.

I asked a Bible study group, composed of women ranging in age from thirty to fifty, to read the material in this chapter and list some of their temptations. Among those listed were pride, anger, impatience (particularly with children), fear, a need to control others, and living beyond their financial means. These are common temptations indeed. Perhaps you struggle with one or more of these temptations yourself. So what are you to do? How can you "attack" temptation at first thought? You do so, as mentioned previously, by yielding to the Holy Spirit—who comes to live within you the moment you accept your redemption through Jesus Christ. The only trouble is that the human will is stubborn and the flesh is weak. It requires continual and deliberate effort to subordinate your will and your earthly desires to God's will and desires—to submit your life moment by moment to the authority of your Master, Redeemer, and Savior: Jesus Christ. The key lies in pursuing and nurturing a relationship with Jesus—not occasionally or as the need arises, but *daily, regularly.* Two of the best ways I know to do this are through spending time in prayer and in reading God's Word.

Prayer. One of my own temptations is to take on more than I can do effectively, so that often I am left feeling frustrated, harried, and overwhelmed. When I analyze this tendency, I wonder if it comes from the low self-esteem that characterized my earlier years and made me a people-pleaser. Through the years, as I've come to understand and embrace my Christian heritage, my self-esteem has been greatly strengthened; and, with the help of Christ, I have been able to do many things with confidence and joy (Philippians 4:13). Yet this debilitating inclination to over-schedule myself still is hard to escape. For years, it was so habitual that I would do it almost automatically. The good news is that I am learning to "attack" this temptation by choosing not to reply immediately but to get back to the person making the request. In the meantime, I pray and listen for an answer to this question: "Lord, what are the important issues here, and what do you want me to do?"

One way I have learned to see the situation objectively and to listen for guidance is to make a list of pros and cons about accepting an invitation. I then pray for direction before I go to sleep. Usually by morning, I have a strong inner assurance that one way or the other is right. If the decision is of real significance—especially when it affects the lives of others—I ask my prayer partner to pray for me to make the right decision. Sometimes I wrestle with the decision for two or three days before I have peace about the direction I will take. When, on rare occasions, the deadline for a decision arrives and I still am not sure, I simply go with my best judgment. After all, 95 percent of the guidance we need has already been given in the Scriptures—especially in the life, teachings, and spirit of Jesus Christ. Only 5 percent of our decisions will require our "wrestling." Once I have completed this process, then—and only then—I act. In this way I am able to order my life according to God's plan instead of my own plan or that of someone else.

I have a friend who is guilty of living beyond her financial means. She is not trying to keep up with the Joneses but attempting to overcome memories of a childhood of poverty and deprivation. Yet she is learning to "attack" the temptation to overspend by spending more time with the One who can "do exceeding abundantly above all that we ask or think" (Ephesians 3:20, KJV). Through prayer, she is learning to trust God's extravagant love and God's ability to provide for all her needs.

A number of years ago, while speaking in our church, Dr. E. Stanley Jones suggested that one of the best ways to overcome temptation is through prevention. He used the illustration of a married man who was physically attracted to a female member of his office staff. Because the man believed in faithfulness in marriage and wanted to preserve his Christian home, Dr. Jones advised him to "nip the temptation in the bud." He suggested that the man should never allow himself to work alone with the woman after hours or even to have a luncheon meeting with just the two of them.

In the case of the woman whose temptation is overspending, she might avoid the shopping mall—and even catalogs and shopping Websites on the Internet. Going to a specific store for a specific purpose would help eliminate the temptation to buy impulsively. She also might shop with an accountability partner, who not only would remind her of her specific purpose but also would serve as a distraction. In fact, an accountability partner is a good idea for anyone struggling with a strong or obsessive temptation.

Of course, the best way to face the dilemma of temptation is to have a vital prayer life. When we live in daily fellowship with

Christ, "the Vine" (John 15:1-5), he will strengthen and empower us through the Holy Spirit; for as he said, "Apart from me you can do nothing" (John 15:5).

God's Word. For many years after I became a Christian, I didn't realize the power of God's Word—especially the Gospels—to transform, empower, and energize us. Despite taking a college course that presented an overview of the Bible, I would only read God's Word devotionally—one verse included in a short devotional reading. Although this practice was (and is) helpful, I discovered that joining a Bible study group and participating in a serious study of the Scriptures allowed me to see God's purposes clearly revealed in my life. Suddenly the life, death, and resurrection of Jesus, the Christ, as a part of the redemptive plan for the world overwhelmed me with God's love. The teachings of Jesus began to make more sense to me and to speak dramatically to my own situations.

If you haven't been involved in a serious study of the Bible, check with your pastor or church staff to find a course or program that's right for you. If none is regularly available, read the Gospel of John along with related study material or commentary. You can use a study Bible or purchase a Bible commentary from a local Christian bookstore. As you do this, you will see that temptation is common to us all—as it was even to Jesus. You also will learn how Jesus achieved victory in the desert—on the "Mount of Temptation"—through the power of God's Word (read Luke 4:1-13). You will see that when Jesus was tempted by Satan, Jesus quoted from the Hebrew Scriptures. When Satan told Jesus to turn stones into bread, Jesus' response included words from Deuteronomy 8:3: "It is written, 'One does not live by bread alone' " (Luke 4:4). When Satan said that the kingdoms of the world would belong to Jesus if he bowed to Satan, Jesus quoted from Deuteronomy 6:13: "It is written, 'Worship the Lord your God, and serve only him' " (Luke 4:8). When Satan told Jesus to cast himself off the Temple because angels would protect him, Jesus quoted from Deuteronomy 6:16: "It is said, 'Do not put the Lord your God to the test'" (Luke 4:12).

A member of a Bible study group, an attractive divorced woman in her early fifties, said that she had no problem resisting sex outside of marriage with casual acquaintances; but she feared that if she ever fell in love, she might not be able to resist the temptation. In addition to having fellowship daily with Christ through prayer, she regularly read the Bible and used scriptural affirmations such as "I can do all things through [Christ] who strengthens me" (Philippians 4:13) and "God did not give us a spirit of cowardice, but rather a spirit of power and of love and of self-discipline" (2 Timothy 1:7).

Why is it so hard for us to resist temptation? Is it possible that we are more like Eve than we ever believed possible? Are we immensely pleased at the thought of being "like God"—of being the one in control, the one in authority? The apostle Paul said, "I die every day!" (1 Corinthians 15:31). In other words, every morning we must remember we are not our own. We were bought with a price. George MacDonald, a nineteenth-century Scottish author who was a strong influence on C. S. Lewis, once said: "The one principle of hell is—'I am my own.'" Once we realize the necessity of daily relinquishment, we are freed to experience the power of God's Word.

I have learned to use biblical affirmations not only when I am tempted but also when I am frightened (2 Timothy 1:7), when I lack confidence (Philippians 4:1-13), when I am anxious (Isaiah 26:3), when I am lonely (Matthew 28:20), when I need courage (Romans 8:37), when I need hope (2 Corinthians 13:11), when I don't feel thankful (Psalm 118:24 and 1 Thessalonians 5:18), and when my faith is weak (Matthew 19:26 and Proverbs 3:5-6). It helps to memorize these and other verses and repeat them whenever you need them. Instead of negative self-talk, use positive biblical affirmations. It will amaze you how this becomes armor for facing life.

I encourage you to allow God's Word to become a practical part of your everyday experiences—"a lamp unto [your] feet, and a light unto [your] path" (Psalm 119:105, KJV). It will be an opportunity for gaining knowledge about God as well as understanding of how to love God.

Lesson 2: Don't play the blame game.

We have a strong tendency to blame others when we have done something wrong. This tendency to play the "blame game" is as ancient as the garden of Eden and as current as the morning newspaper. Although our excuses may be different from Eve's, they're equally as evasive. We blame our genes, our environment, a difficult spouse, a demanding boss, a rebellious teenager, and so forth. All of these "excuses" may make life more difficult at times, but only we are responsible for our lives. In fact, a major step toward spiritual maturity is learning to take full responsibility for our lives. We must admit our mistakes, seek forgiveness, and, through Christ, return to closeness with the One who created us. The Book of First John reminds us: "If we confess our sins, he who is faithful and just will forgive us our sins and cleanse us from all unrighteousness. If we say that we have not sinned, we make him a liar, and his word is not in us" (1:9-10). Why, then, is it so hard to say, "I'm sorry; I was wrong"?

When I was presenting some seminars at a bank in Georgia, one of the employees who came to talk to me was a thirty-nine-year-old secretary. I noticed that her face had lines of tension and her posture was full of despair. Ostensibly, she came to talk with me about her feeling that she was being left out of office conversations and camaraderie. As we talked, she spoke of recurring headaches, insomnia, and stomach problems. After discovering that she had just had a complete physical checkup, I began to probe about what really was bothering her. It turned out that she was harboring a grudge against her sister, whom she blamed for having manipulated her parents. The sister had received a little more of the family inheritance than she (less than $200).

The incident had happened twenty years earlier, and the accumulated weight of blaming her sister was evident in her bitter spirit, her physical symptoms, and her bad interpersonal relationships. She was not hurting her sister by her reactions, but she was destroying herself.

Her only way out was to forgive her sister and close the door on the past. Her resistance to this suggestion was obvious. Unfortunately, she chose to hold on to blame, either because it was habitual or because she felt justified in feeling that way. She chose to hold on to blame even though she was, and perhaps still is, paying a terrible physical and emotional price—and even though she could be "free" any day of her choosing.

May we always confess our sins and remember what Jesus told us: "Whenever you stand praying, forgive, if you have anything against anyone; so that your Father in heaven may also forgive you your trespasses" (Mark 11:25).

Lesson 3: The laws and ways of God are meant not to punish us or make us unhappy, but to give us peace within.

Despite all our labor-saving devices, the world is full of hurry, noise, and pressure. Studies have proved that stress takes a toll on the human body—from headaches to stomach problems, ulcers, heart attacks, hypertension, and even cancer. A number of years ago, I read a newspaper interview with a forty-seven-year-old New York City executive who had left a six-figure salary and opted for life in the country. Although he occasionally did a bit of consulting from home, he basically stayed out of any business circles. He said he had coped so long that he had run out of cope.

In his book *You Can Get Bitter or Better* (Abingdon Press,

1989), James W. Moore quotes a New York doctor who said that civilization's three major killers are not heart disease, cancer, and accidents. Instead, they are calendars, telephones, and clocks—the tyranny of the fast lane. In such a world, is peace even possible? The answer is "Yes!" In his poem "The Place of Peace," Edwin Markham wrote these lines:

> At the heart of the cyclone tearing the sky
> . . . .
> Is a place of central calm.

Even in our stressed-filled and violent world, we can have a sense of calm as we walk in fellowship with Christ. In my experience, "walking in fellowship with Christ" means beginning the day with him. Before I get out of bed for a cup of coffee and a "quiet time," I condition my mind with gratitude, using two biblical affirmations. The first is Psalm 118:24: "This is the day that the Lord has made; / let us rejoice and be glad in it"; the second is my own paraphrase of Colossians 1:27 from *The New Testament in Modern English* translated by J. B. Phillips (New York: The Macmillan Company, 1958): "The secret is this, Nell Mohney. Christ is alive in you, bringing with him the hope of glorious things to come." Then I ask a simple question: "Lord, what are *we* going to do today?" As I mentally go over my schedule for the day, I try to see it from the eyes and motives of Christ.

This simple exercise "jump-starts" my day and creates the climate in which I will live throughout the day. On rare occasions when I oversleep and don't allow time for this exercise, I am irritable and impatient with myself and others. Even if I don't oversleep but wake up thinking, *I'll never get everything done today*, I feel anxious and hurried.

During the course of every day, I say a special prayer for those I will meet and use "shooting prayers" for those who simply come into my mind. I remember using a "shooting prayer" while waiting at the beauty salon one day during the Christmas season. Everyone was in a hurry, and there was an air of tension in the shop. The source of much of that tension was seated in my stylist's chair. Carolyn was an experienced and much-sought-after stylist, but her client was unhappy and complaining. For the third time, she had asked Carolyn to restyle her hair in a different way. Carolyn, realizing that she was running behind, looked as if she were ready to explode. After having just read a book by Dr. Frank Laubach in which he suggested sending "shooting prayers," I decided to try it. I began beaming silent prayers toward that agitated woman. I prayed that she would be relaxed, knowing that God loved her. I gave thanks that she was kind, gracious, and thoughtful. Then I used a silent biblical quotation: "Let not your heart be troubled" (John 14:1, KJV).

Suddenly, an amazing thing happened. The woman toward whom I had sent the prayer stopped complaining and seemed calm. Then she turned to me and said, "I have reacted badly since I have been here." Then to Carolyn she said, "I apologize, but I just felt so stressed when I came in." After she left, Carolyn turned to me and asked, "What did you do to her?" "I shot her— with prayer," I said with a smile. "Do you mind coming in at 2:00 and 4:30 this afternoon?" Carolyn asked. "I have a couple more clients who need to be 'shot.' " All of us laughed, and the tension was broken.

Before every event of the day, I try to bathe the situation in joyful prayer and gratitude. And in the evening as I prepare for bed, I try consciously to turn loose my concerns for the day. For example, when I take off my earrings, I feel myself turning a concern for a grandchild or a problem at the church over to Christ. In that symbolic act, I actually feel tension draining from my body. Then, in my evening prayers, I say something like this: "Lord, thank you for being with me during the day shift, and I turn the night shift over to you." Often I quote this verse: "He gives sleep to his beloved" (Psalm 127:2).

Paul had many beautiful things to say in his thirteen letters found in the New Testament, but one thing he said over and over again is "in Christ." According to German scholar Adolph Deissman, Paul used the phrase "in Christ"—or comparable phrases such as "in him" and "in the Lord"—more than 160 times. For example: "If anyone is in Christ, there is a new creation: everything old has passed away; see, everything has become new!" (2 Corinthians 5:17). In addition, Paul spoke often in his letters about the importance of guarding our thoughts and making them Christ's: "Let this mind be in you, which was also in Christ Jesus" (Philippians 2:5, KJV); and "Whatever is true, whatever is honorable, whatever is just, whatever is pure, whatever is pleasing, whatever is commendable, if there is any excellence and if there is anything worthy of praise, think about these things" (Philippians 4:8). When we are "in Christ," walking in fellowship with him each day, then we realize the promise of Philippians 4:7: "The peace of God, which surpasses all understanding, will guard your hearts and your minds in Christ Jesus."

Lesson 4: The powerful influence of women is unimaginable.

As women, we have incredible influence, and we can use it for good or for evil. As we study women of the Old Testament, we see that some of them used their influence for evil. Among them were Eve, who tempted Adam to disobey God's command; Potiphar's wife, who had Joseph thrown into prison because he wouldn't surrender to her lustful desiring (Genesis 39:7-20); Zipporah, whose neurotic self-centeredness did not help her husband as he sought to fulfill the biggest mandate of his life (*The Women of the Bible*, Herbert Lockyer, Zondervan Publishing House, 1967, pp. 168–69); and Delilah, who used her beauty and charm to defeat Samson, a man of God

(Judges 16:18). On the other hand, there are wonderful examples of Old Testament women who used their influence for good—for God. Among them were Sarah, who, though she made some mistakes, caught God's dream and helped it become a reality (Genesis 21:1); Jochebed, who reared responsible children and taught them to love God—as evidenced by their dedicated leadership in leading the Israelites out of Egypt and through the wilderness (Exodus 5–Deuteronomy 31); Miriam, who used her influence to put spirit and hope into the Israelites in the wilderness (Exodus 15:20); and Esther, who risked her reputation and very life so that her people might live (Esther 4:14-17).

In the nineteenth and twentieth centuries, there also have been many women who have used their influence for good. Florence Nightingale, for example, went against every custom of the day to use her skills as a nurse and help wounded soldiers in the Crimean War. Later in life, even as an invalid, she counseled doctors and nurses and established the Nightingale Training School for Nurses at St. Thomas Hospital in London. Jane Addams, a leader in many reform movements, founded and ran the first Settlement House in Chicago. In 1931, she received the Nobel Peace Prize for lifetime achievement. Mother Teresa, the diminutive Catholic nun, went to Calcutta to teach in a Catholic school. She lived and worked in the safe refuge of the school until one day when she had to go into the city for an errand. That day changed her life. She saw a person dying on the street without any comfort or care. This was a defining moment for Mother Teresa, who received permission to live among the poor and study nursing. In 1950, she established the religious order of Missionaries of Charity, which established homes for homeless people so that they could die in dignity and love. And can any of us forget Corrie ten Boom? She was a Christian from the Netherlands who, in cooperation with her family, helped seven hundred Jews escape arrest by the Nazis. She was later captured and sent to the Ravensbrook Concentration Camp. When released in 1945, she established rehabilitation homes in Holland and Germany for refugees from the concentration camps. She told the story of the holocaust in her three books and numerous speaking engagements and has blessed us all in the process.

If we commit ourselves to using our influence for good, we can change the world!

Digging a Little Deeper

1. Read Genesis 3:2-6. Did Eve have a choice about whether to eat that piece of fruit? Did Adam? How do you know?
2. What is your biggest temptation today? What are you currently doing to become more victorious over temptation, and what else do you need to do? Give an example for each.
3. Read Genesis 3:11-13. Whom did Adam and Eve blame for their disobedience? Whom or what do you have a tendency to blame when you yield to temptation or make a mistake?
4. Which of the biblical affirmations listed in Lesson 2—or other Bible verses—do you think will be most helpful to you in giving up blame and taking responsibility for your life? Why?
5. How would you explain or illustrate what it means to "walk in fellowship with Christ"? Do you agree that walking in fellowship with Christ allows us to stay calm even in a stress-filled world? Why or why not? Despite our best efforts to walk with Christ, what are some of the challenges or obstacles we face each day? How can we overcome them?
6. Which of the biblical affirmations listed in this chapter do you think have been or will be of most help to you? How do you use or plan to use these affirmations?
7. How is Paul's life an example of one who "walked in fellowship with Christ"? What can we learn from his example?

8. From the examples given of Old Testament women whose influence was good, which most inspire or encourage you? Why?
9. Name the women on a local, national, and/or international level who have inspired you to use your influence for good. Explain.

2.

Sarah

God Got Through to Abraham's Beautiful Wife

Scripture Text: **Genesis 11–23**

Now the Lord was gracious to Sarah as he had said, and the Lord did for Sarah what he had promised.

—Genesis 21:1, NIV

Sarah's Story

Sarah—or Sarai, as she is first introduced to us in the Book of Genesis—must have had extraordinary beauty. Even in her old age, people spoke of her beauty. In Genesis 12:14, we read that "the Egyptians saw that [she] was very beautiful," and she would have been in her late sixties at that time! What's more, she had wealth and a husband, Abram, who adored her. Her hometown of Ur was highly civilized, and its wealthy citizens lived in luxury. The most prosperous were idol makers, and Abram's father was one of the leading idol makers of the city.

Scholars tell us that people of wealth in that day had beautiful homes made of cedar and stone. So I can imagine that Sarai was mistress of a handsome house with highly polished floors—perhaps covered with beautiful Oriental rugs. She must have had many servants, beautiful clothes, and plenty of social events to attend. In today's world, Sarai and Abram would be among the "jet set" or the "rich and famous." They had lived in such a world all their married life. Their only sorrow was that they had no children.

The deity of the citizens of Ur was the moon goddess Nana. So how did God get through to this couple? Though they may have heard the ancient story of Adam and Eve, and perhaps the story of Noah, they had no Scriptures and had heard no sermons about the one true God.

Imagine the scene with me. Abram came home while Sarai was being dressed by her maid for dinner. He called her in a voice of extreme urgency: "Sarai, I must talk with you—*now*." She never had heard that tone of voice from her level-headed, steady, and faithful husband. After quickly slipping into a silk robe, she joined her husband in their ornate but pleasant living room. Looking at him with bewilderment and some anxiety, she asked, "What is it, Abram?"

"God spoke to me, Sarai. As clearly as a man can speak, I heard the voice of God speak to me: 'As for you, leave your land, your relatives, and your father's household for a land I will show you; and I will make of you a great nation'" (Genesis 12:1-2, author's paraphrase).

"A great nation?" said Sarai. "How can that be? I am sixty-five and you are seventy-five, and we have no children."

"I don't understand it either," said Abram, "but I know it was the true God who spoke to me, and I don't dare refuse."

"But where are we going? What kind of home will we have? How long will we be gone? And how can we leave your aging father?"

Patiently, Abram replied, "I don't know the answer to any of your questions. I only know that the true God spoke to me and told me that he would show us the way and would be with us. . . ."

When I read the story of Abraham and Sarah—the names later

given to them by God, and thus the names I will use for the remainder of the chapter—I am impressed by their relationship—one that was unusual for a husband and wife in their day. In a culture in which women were considered chattel, Abraham treated his wife as an equal. Later in the Bible story, we read that she had strong opinions and didn't hesitate to express them (see Genesis 16:5 and Genesis 21:10); yet, in this matter that would turn her world upside down, Sarah was strangely quiet. Perhaps God had "gotten through" to her; perhaps God had spoken to her heart as well as to Abraham's.

Two particular incidents in this Old Testament woman's life have spoken directly to me—not because of the circumstances, but because of the underlying principles they represent. The first has to do with "running ahead of God."

When Sarah and Abraham arrived in Canaan and were settled in their large goat's skin tent, Sarah felt that she was too old to give Abraham a son as God had promised. So she decided to help God along by giving her young Egyptian maid, Hagar, as a concubine to Abraham. This was not an unusual practice in their culture. In fact, as part of any wedding ceremony, the wife promised to give her husband a child (a son, they hoped); and if she were barren, she would allow one of her servants to bear his child.

For many wives, this practice was no big deal since they were in a marriage of convenience anyway. But Abraham and Sarah obviously loved each other deeply; thus, the arrangement resulted in a conflict between the two women. When Hagar became pregnant, she became arrogant and no longer respectful of her mistress. Sarah, in her anger and jealousy, so mistreated Hagar that the girl left. In the desert, Hagar thought she was going to die; but God provided water for her to drink and sent her back to her mistress, commanding that she act with respect and obedience (see Genesis 16:1-11).

When Sarah finally bore a son, there was great rejoicing. God had kept his promise—as God always does. Things seemed to go fairly well between the two women until Sarah's son, Isaac, who now was a little boy, was teased and mistreated by his older half-brother, Ishmael. Well, that did it for Sarah! Full of resentment, she sent Hagar and her son out to the desert to die. Once again, God mercifully provided food for these unfortunate victims of circumstance. God promised Hagar not only that she and Ishmael would live but that Ishmael would become the head of a great nation—the Arabs (see Genesis 21:1-18). How often I have wondered if things might be different in the Middle East today if Sarah had not "run ahead" of God by giving Abraham her maidservant and later reacting in anger and vengeance.

The second incident in Sarah's life that has spoken directly to me is perhaps the hardest story in the Old Testament for most people, particularly mothers, to understand. It is the story of the time when Abraham believed God was calling him to sacrifice his beloved son, Isaac (see Genesis 22). The end of the story is that God did not allow Abraham to harm his son; instead, God provided a ram for the sacrifice. Incidentally, according to historical records, human sacrifice was not practiced by the people of God, though such was practiced in the world around them (*The Story of the Bible* by Walter Russell Bowie, Abingdon Press, 1962, p. 48). Abraham discovered that the one true God does not ask that life and love be destroyed. He also discovered, as did Sarah, that God's grace goes before us for the difficult times and places of life. We often talk about the grace of God; but it helps to understand that God gives us three kinds of grace: redeeming grace, which provides for our salvation; sanctifying grace, which enables us to mature in faith; and prevenient grace, which goes before us to prepare the way. It is prevenient grace I am speaking of here; and for me, this is the underlying principle of the story. You might say that God goes ahead of us, in advance, to prepare us or enable us to handle a particular challenge or crisis. We receive this grace as we trust and stay close to God—just as Sarah did.

The Scriptures do not tell us whether Abraham told Sarah about his plans—before or after he and Isaac climbed the mountain. My guess is that he didn't say anything before they left, but that she intuitively knew something was wrong. I believe this because I, too, have experienced that same kind of motherly intuition—as most mothers do at one time or another. On the day that our twenty-year-old son was involved in the accident that took his life, I felt very restless and apprehensive—an intuitive reaction. I suspect God prepared Sarah's heart to hear the news calmly upon their return and to trust God completely for the rest of her long life.

My assumption that Abraham didn't tell Sarah about his plans in advance is based on my own personal knowledge of a mother's absolute heartbrokenness at the death of a child. To feel that your husband had something to do with it would be unbearable. Abraham learned to trust the one true God completely. Though he didn't know how, he trusted that, as Paul would say later, "all things work together for good for those who love God, who are called according to his purpose" (Romans 8:28). He must have believed that, once again, God's prevenient grace would prepare Sarah's heart for whatever lay ahead.

When our son died, I was devastated. There were times when I felt that I could not endure the pain; but as Jesus promised, the Holy Spirit came to dwell within. His presence did not take away the heartbreak, but it brought me comfort and provided empowerment for everyday living. In my darkest night, I never felt alone. Just as Sarah knew so well, I too discovered that God *can* be trusted!

What Can We Learn From Sarah?

Lesson 1: "Running ahead of God" is never a good idea.

Just as Sarah ran ahead of God, allowing her maid, Hagar, to bear Abraham a son, so also we have a tendency to "run ahead of

God" when we feel that things are not moving fast enough or when we simply want to control circumstances or people. Because God has given us free will, God will not stop our actions; yet neither does God save us from the consequences of those actions. In the case of Sarah and Hagar, those consequences were continuing conflict and jealousy between the two—and ultimately the final separation of them and their children.

I remember an incident that happened a long time ago. Jim, at age twenty-five, was fast becoming one of the town's most successful attorneys. Not only was he brilliant in the courtroom but he also was personable and well liked by the townspeople. He was very active in his church, singing in the chancel choir, teaching in the senior high department, and serving on the administrative board.

His friends were pleased when Jim announced that he was to marry Sheila, a beautiful young woman who often had visited in the home of Jim's parents while she and Jim were in law school together. It seemed an idyllic union. Sheila practiced corporate law, and before their marriage, had agreed to work for a large industry in our town.

Their big difficulty lay in the area of faith and church life. Sheila, although a believer, had been turned off as a young person by some of the high-pressure tactics of teachers who had no tolerance for teenagers' honest doubts. She had come to see the church as a place for nonthinkers. Though she had attended worship with Jim when they were in law school, she had no intention of being active in church life after they were married.

Jim, on the other hand, believed that faith and works are inextricably tied together, and for him that meant church activities. Instead of trusting God to work in Sheila's life and allowing her to get to know and trust the congregation, Jim volunteered the two of them for all kinds of things. She had no time to "ease into" church involvement and no opportunity to find her own niche. As a result, there was great conflict and misunderstanding between them. If they had not received excellent counseling, Jim might have lost his wife; and his church and the kingdom of God might have lost Sheila, who turned out to be a talented and committed disciple of Jesus Christ. Jim "ran ahead of God."

Fortunately, God doesn't get angry and punish us for our impulsive actions. Instead, there is always the option of a way out—one that is never in opposition to God's character. Our responsibility is to see and accept that way out. Perhaps it is pride that makes us feel we must take control of situations; in fact, many Bible scholars say that pride is the root of all other sins. Of course, it is appropriate for us to take the initiative in many situations, but never without praying for direction—and being willing to wait for the answer.

Lesson 2: God never calls us to a task without providing the necessary resources.

Abraham and Sarah, who knew little of God's nature, received God's prevenient grace to prepare their hearts and wills for the gigantic task ahead of them. First, God's prevenient grace prepared Abraham's heart to hear God's call to leave the land of his fathers and to go to a place where God directed. All this happened *before* Abraham knew the Scriptures or was taught about God. Certainly God's prevenient grace prepared Sarah to leave her lovely home in Haran and live in a large goat's skin tent in a foreign land. Later, God prepared the aged Sarah to believe that she would bear a son and that he would be a part of God's plan for redeeming the world. It also is a safe assumption that God prepared Sarah to hear of Isaac's near death because the Bible never again speaks of her anger with her husband or her God. Her heart finally had learned to trust completely this sovereign God.

Perhaps one of the most exciting experiences we can have is to see in retrospect the many times God's prevenient grace has guided our lives and prepared our hearts. In my own life, I realize that I was guided to attend a church-related college—which prepared me for working in the field of Christian Education—rather than the less-expensive state university I had planned to attend. I'm awed when I see how God brought my husband, Ralph, and me together for marriage, and how the doors of service opportunities have been opened to us. God's grace has brought people into my life to help in the different places—and prepared me for allowing them to help. I challenge you to look back and give thanks for God's prevenient grace in your life. Once you do, perhaps you will wonder, as I do, why we ever feel that we have to control situations or to run ahead of God. The truth is, we can't. God's already there, patiently waiting for us.

Lesson 3: God can use what God didn't choose.

Despite our mistakes, if we are willing to seek God's guidance, we will receive God's redeeming grace. God can and does save us—not only from eternal death through sin but also from everyday discouragement, despair, and hopelessness. In other words, God can bring good from bad situations. For example, God provided for Sarah when, through Abraham's cowardice, she was called into Pharaoh's harem (see Genesis 12:10-20). Likewise, God also provided for Hagar and Ishmael in the desert after Sarah asked Abraham to send them away (see Genesis 21:8-19).

Through the years, as Ralph and I have reflected on the death of our twenty-year-old son and the resultant suffering of our family and others, we don't for one minute believe that God caused our son's accident. We believe that God is sovereign, but that God has given us freedom of will. This means that we can harm ourselves and others. Yet God's love and grace can heal our broken hearts and bring triumph out of tragedy. God can indeed use what God did not choose. In our own case, we have been led to minister to those whose children have died. In addition, we have come to understand how fragile life really is, to be grateful for each day, and to treasure all our relationships, especially those with family members.

Once, while visiting in Damascus, Syria, I saw a master weaver who stood before an Oriental rug, directing the weavers on the other side of the rug. When they made a mistake or dropped a stitch, the master weaver changed the pattern somewhat so that the entire rug would be a thing of beauty. In the same way, God can take our mistakes and pain and make something beautiful of our lives. God can use what God did not choose—if we allow it.

Lesson 4: Ultimately, anger and revenge never win.

Sarah learned this lesson the hard way. Her anger and vengeful actions toward Hagar and Ishmael caused conflict in her marriage (see Genesis 21:10-11) and in her home, for anger creates tension in all—especially children who come within the path of anger's destruction. As it is with us, her revenge must have caused dis-ease in her own spirit.

If she hadn't reacted impulsively and emotionally, Sarah could have centered herself in God's sanctifying grace, which allows us to "grow up" in faith. Sanctifying grace also enables us to find peaceful solutions through calm, clear, and prayerful thinking.

On his cassette tape "NeuroCybernetics," Dan Kennedy tells of watching a golf tournament in which Arnold Palmer made a spectacularly bad golf shot. Instead of flying into a rage, Palmer calmly walked over to survey the spot where the ball lay almost buried behind a tree. Placing one foot precariously above the ball and the other below the ball, he took what most people considered an impossible shot. Yet that chip shot seemed to land the ball effortlessly on the green.

At another hole in the same tournament, according to Mr. Kennedy, Tiger Woods made a spectacularly bad shot. Instead of calmly surveying the situation, he reacted emotionally by throwing his club on the ground and yelling at himself for such a stupid shot. His game never fully recovered that day. Of course, part of the difference in their reactions was the difference in their age and maturity. In my observation, Tiger Woods's reactions have steadied with each tournament, and he plays brilliantly today.

The human mind never functions effectively when it is hot with emotion. Only when it is "cool" does it produce those insights, understandings, and dispassionate concepts that lead to a solution. My mother was a living example of this principle. Rather than lose her temper when someone outside the family tried to control or take advantage of one of our family members, she often quoted from Jewell Bothwell Tull's "Coquette," where she writes of lightly holding those you love, for

> Things with wings, held tightly
> Long to go.

It is so true: Uncontrolled anger spoils friendships, destroys marriages, alienates parents and children, and costs many people their jobs. To be angry is not wrong, but to express anger destructively is wrong. When you lose your temper because you are out of control, you are less than God intended you to be. In Proverbs 16:32 we read, "One who is slow to anger is better than the mighty, / and one whose temper is controlled than one who captures a city." The Bible also instructs us, "Be angry but do not sin; do not let the sun go down on your anger" (Ephesians 4:26). In our premarital counseling, the minister who married my husband and me used Paul's quotation from Ephesians 4 to tell us not to go to bed angry. Years later, we laughingly told him that during our first year of marriage, we stayed up later than either of us ever had before! Yet it was a good exercise in working through our conflicts before we knelt to share our evening prayers. When we strive to live according to these biblical guidelines and seek to follow God's purposes, we receive sanctifying grace that enables us to mature in faith, to overcome obstacles, and to live in peace and power as people of God.

Nothing is more beautiful than a life lived under God's control. Once Michaelangelo was asked, "When is a painting finished?" He replied, "When it fulfills the intent of the artist." On a similar note, a life is "finished" or complete when one's life fulfills the intent of the Creator. Though she obviously had some obstacles to face, including her anger and bitterness toward Hagar, Sarah ultimately was able to overcome them with God's help and be a "grace-full" participant in God's great plan. Without a doubt, her life was "complete" in God's sight.

Digging a Little Deeper

1. Read Genesis 16:1. How did Sarah "run ahead" of God?
2. Have you ever run ahead of God? If so, how? Why do you think we so often want to control the people and events around us?
3. How do you think you would react if your spouse or loved one announced to you that God had called him or her to leave a comfortable lifestyle and move far away? Try to answer as honestly as you can. In what ways has God called you to step out of your "comfort zone"? How have you responded?
4. After reading the story of Abraham and Sarah (Genesis 11–23), in what ways do you see God's prevenient grace preparing their hearts for the tasks ahead?
5. Think/tell of a time when you were aware of God's prevenient grace, which goes before us to prepare the way. How did God provide for your needs at this time?
6. How did God bring good out of the following situations: when Sarah was called into Pharaoh's harem (Genesis 12:10-20);

when Sarah had Abraham sent Hagar and Ishmael into the desert (Genesis 21:8-19).

7. Tell how God brought good out of a difficult situation in your life or the life of someone you know.

8. Read Genesis 16:1 and 21:8-20. Discuss how life could have been different for Sarah if she hadn't "run ahead" of God, then exploded in anger at Hagar.

9. What pushes your "hot buttons"? How do you manage your anger? Write a prayer, asking God for the help you need. Be as honest and specific as you can.

3.

$\mathcal{K}$eturah

Blueprint for a Second Wife

Scripture Text: **Genesis 25:1-4; 1 Chronicles 1:32-33**

Abraham took another wife, whose name was Keturah. She bore him Zimran, Jokshan, Medan, Midian, Ishbak, and Shuah.

—Genesis 25:1-2

Keturah's Story*

Second wives—theirs is not the most enviable position, whether the first wife died or there was a divorce. After a marriage has ended and the period of grief has passed, memories of the first wife, whether good or bad, tend to get exaggerated. I love the story about a minister who, while preaching a sermon about marriage, emphasized that we all have made mistakes in marriage. On impulse, he turned to his small congregation and asked, "Does anyone here believe that you have been a perfect mate?" Most of the people smiled at the thought, but one short, mild-mannered man raised his hand. The stunned pastor asked,

---

* The story of Keturah in this chapter is based upon my own imagination and information found in the following sources: Herbert Lockyer, *The Women of the Bible* (Grand Rapids, Mich.: Zondervan Publishing House, © 1967); Joan Comay, *Who's Who in the Old Testament* (Nashville: Abingdon Press, A Festival Book, © 1971); Edith Deen, *All the Women of the Bible* (New York: Harper & Brothers Publishers, © 1955); Edith Deen, *Families Living in the Bible* (New York: Harper & Brothers Publishers, © 1963).

"Oh, you believe that you have been a perfect husband, Mr. Madison?" The soft-spoken man replied, "No, but according to my wife, her first husband was." After the laughter ceased, no doubt most of the congregation thought, *What a terrible burden to lay on a second spouse.*

Once I overheard a second wife give the following advice to a woman who was about to become a second wife: "Acknowledge the past, but don't dwell on it, and live in the present." If both partners are widowed, they should take equal responsibility for practicing that advice. If one partner has never been married before, the responsibility falls more heavily, I believe, on the formerly married spouse.

In the case of Abraham, it must have been hard for him to follow that advice. After all, he was 137 years old when Sarah died at age 127! And he didn't marry again until his son, Isaac, was safely married to Rebekah, who was from their home country. Though we are not sure how many years passed before Isaac and Rebekah were married, we do know that Abraham was 175 when he died. "Impossible," you may say, but even at the beginning of this century, there are some 70,000 centenarians living in America alone (according to the Huffington Center on Aging, Baylor College of Medicine, Houston, Texas). When you consider that in Abraham's day there were no modern-day stresses, no pollution, and no processed foods, his advanced age doesn't seem so impossible after all.

Abraham's second wife, Keturah, is said to have been a young woman when they married (Herbert Lockyer, *The Women of the Bible*; Zondervan Publishing House, 1967; p. 82). We can only imagine what Keturah might have experienced with this lonely, old man who had adored his beautiful first wife, for the Bible tells us very little. Yet we can combine what other sources tell us about her with our own creative reasoning to get a fairly good picture of Keturah (see list of sources on page 45).

Keturah, a Hittite, had grown up as the second of four daughters and one son born to Ishbak and his wife, Moriah. She wasn't beautiful—her features were too large for her small head and face. Her hair was not raven black and curly like that of her three sisters. In fact, even her younger sisters were married before she. Yet Keturah was young and firm of body, and she had a deep longing for home and family. In her youth, she had imagined herself married to a tall, handsome, and brave lover who would hold her in his strong arms and proudly bring home the venison he had shot in the plains. Actually, there were two young suitors whom she could have married. Her father, Ishbak, approved of both and was irritated by her adamant refusal. He could have insisted, and she would have had to obey; but he had a strong affection for this daughter with a kind, compassionate heart. Since early childhood, she had followed a different path—aware of a God none of the rest of them knew.

Somehow her father was not surprised that she seemed attracted to the aged and widowed Abraham, who had come to their country long ago as a foreigner from Haran. He was a follower of one he called "the true God." Many in the land of Canaan also had become followers because of the strength of character they found in this righteous man. Ishbak knew that Keturah spent hours in the tent of Abraham's wife, Sarah, asking questions about the God who called them out from their homeland. Keturah truly mourned Sarah's death. In fact, Sarah had become a role model for the young woman. Keturah admired Sarah's independent spirit, her laughter and love of life, and her commitment to the God who had asked so much of them.

After Abraham's period of mourning had passed, Ishbak invited the lonely man to have an evening meal with his family. They all enjoyed hearing Abraham's stories of living in Haran, of heeding God's call, and of making the long journey to Canaan. Ishbak noticed that Keturah was listening with rapt attention. He could feel her compassionate heart going out to this grieving man. Abraham reciprocated Ishbak's dinner invitation, and their meals together became habitual.

Over the following months, Ishbak became aware of Abraham's growing interest in Keturah; but even he was surprised when the aged Abraham asked for Keturah's hand in marriage. I can imagine the kind of exchange that must have taken place later between this father and daughter.

"Abraham is old," Ishbak said, "and you will spend your youth caring for an ailing man."

Keturah answered respectfully but pragmatically: "I know that, father, but there are two things you overlook: I love Abraham and would care for him gladly. Also, he has the moral strength and righteousness I have always wanted in a husband."

Ishbak nodded and added, "I know it will be easy for you to follow his God."

With dancing eyes, Keturah replied, "Oh, father, from Sarah I learned about the true God, and I have followed the true God for years."

And so, after Isaac and Rebekah were married, Keturah became Abraham's second wife.

We know little about their life together except that Keturah bore Abraham six sons and cared for him until his death at 175 years of age. We also know that Sarah always was first in Abraham's life because, though he bestowed gifts on Keturah's sons, his inheritance was left to Sarah's son, Isaac (Genesis 25:5-6). Yet Keturah has much to teach all of us—both men and women, single or married. In particular, however, she speaks to persons living in blended families, who are challenged with one of the most difficult forms of family life. When you combine the difficulties facing couples in second marriages with the additional difficulties of nurturing children in a blended family, the result is a tremendously challenging form of family life, indeed. And when you consider the prediction that by the year 2005, more Americans will be living in blended families than in traditional families (*20/20* special report on blended families, June 1998), it is even more clear that Keturah really is speaking to us all!

What Can We Learn From Keturah?

Lesson 1: Negative emotions such as jealousy, insecurity, fear, and anger will destroy a marriage.

This is true in any marriage—whatever the "number"! If you are insecure or jealous, have a need to be the best in everything, or are vengeful, you shouldn't become a "second spouse." Your life—and your spouse's life—will be miserable! Perhaps this is why so many second marriages do not work. Sometimes the first spouse sows the seeds of dissent by angrily anticipating her or his spouse's remarriage.

I once read of a first wife who was terminally ill and decided to have her portrait painted. When the artist had almost completed the portrait of the woman wearing an emerald-colored evening gown, the woman casually remarked that she wanted him to paint a glittering emerald and diamond necklace at her neckline, with matching earrings on her ears. "Oh, I didn't know you had such jewelry," remarked her artist friend. "I don't," replied the woman, "but I want my husband's second wife to think I did and drive herself crazy looking for it." We may laugh about this, but within her attitude was the hope of an unhappy second marriage for her husband.

Just as jealously, insecurity, fear, and anger can destroy a marriage, so also there are positive attributes that help to hold a marriage together. Though we have few biblical facts about Keturah, there are enough "clues" to help us understand some important attributes for a Christian wife—especially a second wife.

First, she possesses self-understanding. Keturah must have known herself well enough to know that she could be happy with an older man, for whom she would have to be the primary caregiver.

It is really hard to know ourselves. Benjamin Franklin once wrote: "Three things are hard in this world: steel, diamonds, and learning to know oneself." In my own life, it took me a number of years to understand the source of some of my insecurities and fears. Since husbands and wives come from different backgrounds, it is important for us to see these clearly. I suggest that we do some prayerful introspection in order to identify our insecurities and fears, and having done this, that we list them on paper so that we may understand our spouse's reactions and the perspective from which he or she sees the world.

Second, she respects and appreciates herself because she is created by God, redeemed by Christ, and empowered by the Holy Spirit. Because of this confidence, she is not as dependent upon and sensitive to the reactions of others, even those close to her.

Third, she has respect for her spouse and every person within the family circle—stepchildren as well as biological or adopted children. That doesn't mean that she always likes them; she doesn't! But she always respects them and never attacks them with words aimed at their most vulnerable points.

Fourth, she remembers that marriage was God's idea (Genesis 2:1-24) and that marriage was blessed by Jesus in Cana of Galilee (John 2:1-11). If she and her family are seeking to walk in God's way through Christian faith, there always is a workable solution. Thus, she works to handle conflict creatively. She also is able to communicate her own feelings and desires without destructive anger.

Fifth, she knows the crucial importance of continuing to show affection and appreciation for her husband and children. This means giving understanding and encouragement. In regards to her husband, it also means that she knows the importance of sex. I once heard the Christian author Josh McDowell say that in college he took "Marriage 101" from an eighty-one-year-old professor who was much loved on campus. One day a student asked, "When do you lose interest in sex?" The professor smiled as he said, "I don't know. It's sometime after eighty-one." Sometimes, as Christians, we may forget that God created sex as the deepest form of communication—physical, mental, emotional, and spiritual—between a husband and wife who are committed in love to each other. There shouldn't be boredom in the bedroom!

Sixth, since all of us make mistakes, a wife should practice forgiveness as she has received forgiveness from Christ. In the final analysis, it is Christian forgiveness in love that holds a marriage together.

Seventh, both she and her husband make Christ the "head" of their home. The marriage relationship is like a triangle, with Christ at the apex and the husband and wife at the two corners. The closer they move, individually, toward Christ, the closer they are to each other.

Though I have suggested that these seven attributes are important for Christian wives, they are equally relevant for Christian husbands. To be sure, marriage is a partnership requiring the work of both spouses. And, with Christ at the center, it can be a successful, lasting partnership.

Lesson 2: A second wife should recognize, acknowledge, and respect the past, yet always live in the present.

Keturah respected and admired Abraham's first wife, Sarah. My guess is that she never tried to avoid the subject when Abraham discussed one of his memories of Sarah or of their time together. But I also imagine that Keturah made her life with Abraham so interesting and exciting, he had less and less need to talk of his first wife. And I suspect Keturah's ability to respect the past while living in the present was a key to their happiness together.

I can't think of Keturah without thinking of my friend Mildred, who married her best friend's husband after her friend's death. Mildred and Aletha had worked together and had become friends soon after Aletha and Thad were married. It wasn't long before Mildred moved to another part of the country, and she and Aletha saw each other only on holidays and vacation visits. Through the years, Mildred had a number of suitors, but she never married; she enjoyed her career and the opportunity she had for travel.

After Mildred's father died and her mother's health began to decline, she took early retirement and returned to her hometown to care for her mother. For the next several years, Mildred and Aletha met weekly for lunch and shopping. Then, after Aletha died, her husband, Thad, was consumed by grief. Even though my husband, Ralph, and I had moved to another city, we kept in touch with Thad and noticed the changes taking place. He lost weight, his health declined, and he lacked his usual enthusiasm for his two chief interests: his business and his church. Ralph commented once that he didn't think Thad would live for a year.

Thad's friends and neighbors saw the changes, too, and they tried to help by involving him in activities and bringing him food. Mildred and her mother invited him over occasionally for a home-cooked meal. Soon, he was looking and feeling much better. Then Mildred began to attend activities with him. More than a year after Aletha's death, we were back in town for a meeting in the church where my husband had served as senior pastor for many years, and we went to see Thad. He told Ralph he was going to ask Mildred to marry him, and he asked Ralph what he thought about it. Even to this day Mildred says laughingly that Thad asked Ralph before he asked her!

Ralph and I were present for the small but beautiful wedding and the luncheon that followed. We are convinced that Thad's happiness with Mildred was what kept him alive for eight more years. Our friendship with Thad and Mildred was as strong as our friendship with Thad and Aletha had been. We often ate together, traveled together, and worshiped together. After Thad's death, our friendship with Mildred, a remarkable woman, continues to this day.

One of the things I noticed when we visited in Thad and Mildred's home soon after their marriage was that Mildred had as many pictures of Thad and Aletha on display as pictures of Thad and herself. The two of them spoke of Aletha as naturally as they told of their latest trip. Perhaps most telling of all was that Mildred buried Thad beside his first wife, and she has continued his philanthropy in the way he would have liked.

In the eight years Thad and Mildred were married, we never observed in Mildred even the slightest hint of self-pity or a "second fiddle" attitude. She was an independent woman who seemed to enjoy thoroughly her marriage to a man fifteen years her senior, yet she always showed respect and appreciation for his first wife. I believe that all this was possible because she is a committed Christian, is positive and unselfish, and believes in living in the present.

One of the most difficult skills we must learn is to turn loose the "baggage" of the past. Yet we must learn the lesson well if we are to live *fully* in God's present.

Digging a Little Deeper

1. Negative emotions are hard on any relationship, especially a marriage. The negative emotion we express most often is anger, which prevents us from effectively expressing our real feelings. Anger is clinically called "a secondary emotion"; it

masks a primary emotion such as fear or loss or grief. Think of a time recently when you were angry. What primary emotion was your anger masking? How did you handle your anger? What might you do differently "next time"?

2. Read Genesis 4:1-12. What was Cain's primary emotion? Why did he kill his brother, Abel? What does God tell Cain about his offering (verses 5-7)?

3. Read Matthew 21:12-13. Why was Jesus angry? Is it wrong to be angry? When and how can anger become a destructive emotion?

4. Read Ephesians 4:26-27. What does Paul suggest is the right time limit for dealing with anger? Why is it important not to go to bed angry? What can happen when we allow conflict to go unresolved?

5. Read Proverbs 16:32 and James 1:19. What wisdom regarding anger do we gain from these verses?

6. What pushes your "hot buttons"? How do you control your anger?

7. Consider/discuss the following "plan" for handling anger:
   • Recognize and acknowledge points of personal vulnerability; then be on guard against anger when someone invades those points of vulnerability.
   • Since childish patterns of behavior quickly pop up when we are under pressure, try to recognize and put away some of those childish things in advance (see 1 Corinthians 13:11).
   • When anger and conflict arise, use a three-step strategy:
   1) Go away from the situation for a short time to pray and cool off.
   2) Write down what the issue really is and try to see it from the other person's point of view.
   3) Get back together as quickly as possible to discuss and try to resolve the conflict. Try to put your pride aside; being "right" is not the loving answer to any argument. Offer for-

giveness, remembering that the Lord has forgiven you. Work out a compromise if possible. If not, be willing to disagree; it's okay to think differently. Always end an argument with some form of physical touch: a hug, a kiss, or even a touch on the arm or shoulder. Always remember that no one can make you angry. You *choose* to be angry.

8. There are three primary emotions that are extremely difficult to handle, especially in close relationships: fear, jeaousy, and resentment. Which of these do you deal with most often? What does the Bible tell us about it? Use a Bible concordance to find passages that speak to this emotion. (When looking for passages on *fear*, we also can look for passages on *anxiety* and *worry*, because both are fear thoughts that go round and round in the same groove in our minds, much like a broken record.)

9. How can you overcome your fears? Consider/discuss the following suggestions:
   • Fight your fears with prayer and proactive thinking. Remember that fears are thoughts, and you can change your thought patterns. If the fears are deep seated, you may need the help of a counselor to discover their roots.
   • Rather than fretting about your fears, act courageously, with the help of God, to overcome them. Teddy Roosevelt is reported to have said: "I have often been afraid, but I wouldn't give in to it. I have made myself act as if I were not afraid and gradually the fear disappeared." Likewise, Emerson reminds us: "Do the thing you fear, and the death of fear is certain."
   • Repeat this powerful affirmation: "I can do all things through [Christ] who strengthens me" (Philippians 4:13). This scriptural affirmation calms our spirits, reminding us that we are not alone. (Also see "Affirmations for the Journey Ahead," page 57.)

10. Respond to the following: Jealousy is the backwash of per-

sonal insecurity; at its core is envy—the pain or annoyance felt at the happiness of another.

11. How can you overcome jealousy? Consider/discuss the following suggestions:
    • Work on your self-image. Remember that we are created in the image of God (Genesis 1:27) and that all of us have broken the image (Romans 3:23); still, we have been redeemed by Jesus Christ (John 3:16), and we are empowered by the Holy Spirit (John 1:12). Affirm yourself as a person of worth because of what Christ has done for you. (See "Affirmations for the Journey Ahead," page 57.)
    • Keep a journal so that you may see your progress and identify areas that still need work.
    • Remember that only the Great Physician is equal to our need. We must turn to Christ and learn to develop his thought patterns (see Philippians 2:5).
    • Remember that we are all Christians under construction. God's sanctifying grace is working on us every day. Our job is to cooperate with God, live in fellowship with Christ, and know that "the one who began a good work among you will bring it to completion" (Philippians 1:6).
    • Discover the unique, God-given plan for your life through prayer, Bible study, and worship (see Jeremiah 29:11).

12. Respond to the following: Resentment is like a splinter that gets under your skin. Unless it is removed, it will cause infection.

13. How can you overcome resentment? Consider/discuss the following suggestions:
    • Decide that you will turn resentment loose. Resentment in your spirit will cause bitterness, anger, cynicism, loss of enthusiasm and joy, and even physical illness. Holding a grudge against someone won't hurt that person, but it will destroy you.

• Consider seeking a "care-frontation," in which you seek reconciliation with the person you resent.
• Ask for forgiveness and make restitution (see Mark 11:25).
• Move on with your life.

14. Read Matthew 6:12. Think about past hurts in your relationships—particularly a relationship in which you are/were married. Do you need to forgive someone and/or be forgiven? Do you need to forgive yourself?

15. After considering the material in this chapter and reading the Scripture text given for the chapter (see page 45), how do you think Keturah was able to acknowledge Abraham's past yet live in the present?

16. Read Genesis 25:5-6. If you were Keturah, how would you have felt about Abraham leaving the largest part of his inheritance to Sarah's son? Why?

17. As a Christian, what "resources" would most help you in achieving happiness in marriage? Why? What are the important "everyday resources" available to all Christians?

Affirmations for the Journey Ahead

The following affirmations helped me tremendously as I sought to move from a negative, pessimistic self-image to a confident self-image that encourages me to grow in self-confidence and to become what God has called me to be. Say one or more of the following affirmations when you first awaken. They also may be used anytime you are feeling inferior or inadequate.

"I can do all things through [Christ] who strengthens me" (Philippians 4:13).

"If God is for us, who is against us?" (Romans 8:31).

"Be patient with me. God hasn't finished with me yet."

"The one who began a good work among you will bring it to completion" (Philippians 1:6).

"This is the day that the LORD has made; / let us rejoice and be glad in it" (Psalm 118:24).

4.

Jochebed

Imparting Character, Wisdom, and Faith to Our Children

Scripture Text: **Numbers 26:59; Exodus 1; 2:1-11**

The name of Amram's wife was Jochebed daughter of Levi, who was born to Levi in Egypt; and she bore to Amram: Aaron, Moses, and their sister Miriam.

—Numbers 26:59

Jochebed's Story

"Tell us the story again," begged three-year-old Aaron and seven-year-old Miriam as Jochebed was hearing their prayers. Though her heart was heavy, Jochebed told the story again to remind them of their heritage and to help them believe that the one true God would send someone to deliver them from slavery in Egypt.

Even as she told the story, her own faith was rekindled and her heart felt a bit lighter. "Once there was a little Hebrew boy named Joseph who lived in Canaan with his father and his eleven brothers. The brothers were jealous of him because he seemed to be their father's favorite. His father had given him a coat of many colors, which they envied. So when Joseph delivered food to his brothers in the field, they took the coat and sold him to a caravan of Midianites going to Egypt.

"In Egypt, Joseph was bought by Potiphar, an Egyptian officer and captain of the guard. Later, Joseph became governor of Egypt. When there was a famine in Canaan, his brothers came asking the governor for food. They didn't recognize Joseph, but he knew them. Already he had forgiven them, and he brought his father and his eleven brothers and their families to live in Egypt. They were very happy there; but as the years went by, the number of Hebrews grew large. A new pharaoh came to power, and he decided to make the Hebrews slaves."

"Why?" asked Aaron solemnly, as if he had never asked it before.

"You know why," said Miriam, as she tossed her dark curls. "He was afraid that there would be more Hebrews than Egyptians, so he took our freedom away. But God will send someone to set us free." Then, as she turned to her mother and looked directly into her eyes, Miriam asked, "Mother, is it true that the pharaoh has ordered all newborn Hebrew baby boys to be killed?"

Getting up quickly so as not to allow the children to see the fear on her face, the very pregnant Jochebed answered quietly, "Yes."

But Miriam persisted. "Is that why we have heard women screaming at night?"

As she walked away, Jochebed said, "Perhaps."

"Wait, mother. What if our new baby is a boy? What will we do?" Miriam continued. By now Miriam's voice indicated the terrible dread that she had internalized and kept hidden from her parents.

Quickly, Jochebed returned to the children, sat down by their beds, and said very calmly, "If this should happen, we will do what we have always done in a crisis. We will be calm, think clearly, and trust God to guide us."

Even as she kissed her children good night, Jochebed's labor pains had begun. Perhaps her children's fears had ceased, but her turmoil had just begun.

Now, more than thirty centuries later, we know that Jochebed's baby was a boy and that his name was Moses (Exodus 2:1-10). This remarkable Hebrew woman didn't react as her neighbors had. There were no emotional hysterics, no screaming. Rather, she followed her own advice to be calm, to think clearly, and to trust God for guidance.

There is no record of where Jochebed hid her beautiful baby boy for three months (Exodus 2:2). Neither do we know at what point God gave her the idea to hide the child in a basket in the Nile at the very hour and spot where the pharaoh's daughter came daily to bathe. My guess is that she must have worked feverishly to weave a basket of bulrushes from the pliant stems of the papyrus plant.

Young Miriam watched hour by hour as her mother completed the basket and lined it with pitch and tar to make it watertight. Can't you imagine that as Miriam watched her mother work day after day, Jochebed was carefully rehearsing the seven-year-old's part in the plan?

"This is your job, Miriam. No one else can do it, and you may have to wait in the bulrushes for a long time. But you must be quiet and not move to any other place. Are you ready, Miriam?"

Miriam's eyes must have danced in excitement each day as she replied, "I am ready!"

Finally the day arrived! Jochebed placed the basket in the water. She stationed Miriam nearby, hidden by the bulrushes. When Pharaoh's daughter arrived, her maidens walked along the banks to find a shallow area for her bath. Then she spotted the basket and asked a slave girl to retrieve it. When the princess opened the basket, she exclaimed, "It's one of the Hebrew babies!" That was Miriam's cue. She ran to Pharaoh's daughter and asked, "Shall I go get one of the Hebrew women to nurse the baby for you?"

Obviously, there was nothing suspicious about Miriam's manner or inquiry, because the princess immediately replied, "Yes, go." Quickly, Miriam returned to her mother who was standing a little distance back—and probably giving thanks that the God-given idea was working. Pharaoh's daughter asked Jochebed to nurse the child and return him to her when he was older. She would pay Jochebed well for this task. During those early years, Jochebed loved her son and taught him, as she had her other two children, about his heritage and the true God whom they served. God's plan to deliver his people was being set in motion. When the little boy was returned to the princess, it was she who named him Moses, saying, "I drew him out of the water" (Exodus 2:10).

Jochebed's name is mentioned only twice in the Bible (Numbers 26:59 and Exodus 6:20), but thirty-three hundred years after her death, her name is still remembered as one of the great mothers of history.

What Can We Learn From Jochebed?

Lesson 1: Nothing in life is more important than imparting character, wisdom, and faith to the children in our lives.

We never get very far from the early years of our rearing. The instruction we receive as young children goes with us throughout life—safely "tucked away" in the personalities we develop and carry around for a lifetime, as well as in our memories. Certainly this is evident in the life of Moses, Aaron, and Miriam. God used their godly Hebrew mother to impart wisdom, character, and faith in her children. Though it's likely she didn't live long enough to see God's plan accomplished, Jochebed prepared her children well for the gigantic, historical task God had in mind.

Mothers, fathers, and grandparents—and, for that matter, aunts, uncles, and neighbors—all of us are teachers, whether we want to be or not. As a young mother, I used to be haunted by a poem thought to be written by a public school teacher:

Sculpture

I took a piece of plastic clay
And idly fashioned it one day.
And as my fingers pressed it still,
It moved and yielded to my will.
I came again when days were past.
That bit of clay was hard at last.
The form I gave it, still it bore,
And I could change it never more.

I took a piece of human clay
And gently formed it day by day.
I molded with my power and art
A young child's soft and yielding heart.
I came again when years were gone,
It was a man I looked upon.
He still that early impress bore,
And I could change it never more.

Whatever else we accomplish in life, nothing is more important than imparting character, wisdom, and faith to our children—and to all the young lives we may touch.

Lesson 2: We must not allow our emotions to rule us.

Emotions are a wonderful part of our human makeup. They express our feelings: fear, love, anger, compassion, hatred, hope, kindness, joy. Without them, we would be ruled only by logic, which can be unfeeling and sometimes grim. Yet emotions can be destructive when allowed to get out of control.

Our emotions are like gasoline in a car's engine. Without gasoline, the engine cannot do what it was built to do; gasoline gives it the "get up and go" to start moving. But if the gasoline is inflamed by fire or an explosion, it destroys the car that it was designed to move forward. In his book *Ride the Wild Horses!* the late Dr. J. Wallace Hamilton used another analogy for emotions; he called them "wild horses." He said that either we tame them, or they destroy us.

Jochebed was well aware of the destructive nature of uncontrolled emotions. Her very name means "Jehovah is our glory" (Herbert Lockyer, *The Women of the Bible*, Zondervan Publishing House, Grand Rapids, Michigan, 1967), and she lived up to her name. Through the guidance of Jehovah, she was able to control her emotions when crisis came—to stay calm, to think clearly, and to trust God for the future.

Let me tell you the story of two attractive young couples. During her third pregnancy, one wife discovered, rather inadvertently, that her husband had had a "one-night stand" with a woman of questionable character. The wife went into hysterics, which went on and on. She frightened and neglected her children. She put her husband out of the house and discredited him to anyone who would listen to her tirades. The young man sought reconciliation, but the horses of her emotions were running wild. Finally, the husband left town, leaving his children fatherless and his wife an embittered woman. Sadly, all three children developed serious problems that have lasted throughout their adult lives.

The second family had just the opposite experience. They, too, were a young couple with two children. It was widely rumored in the community that the husband was having an affair with a young widow, yet you never would have known it by observing his wife. She, like Jochebed, stayed calm, thought clearly, and sought guidance from God.

The end of the story is that the affair ended and the couple stayed together, attended church with their children, and reared two fine young people. What was the difference?

When an acquaintance told the wife of the rumors, she replied, "I simply don't believe that. Jim is not a womanizer." But she very wisely began to look for signs—staying late at the office, being unavailable during lunch time, and so forth. Although her natural instinct was to panic when she began to notice a few signs, she didn't react emotionally. Instead, she thought calmly and objectively about the situation, remembering what a loving husband and father Jim was. Still, although she didn't have concrete evidence of the affair, she intuitively knew that the rumors were true. She didn't deny the truth; but instead of reacting emotionally and impulsively, she chose to look at the "big picture" before choosing a course of action.

First, she began to analyze her own behavior. In her busyness with young children and multiple church and community activities, she had put Jim's needs last. "There was boredom in the bedroom," she said. "Even my nightwear was no longer romantic. It was easy to slip into something comfortable but bedraggled." Then she thought of the widow named in the rumors. Already the woman had come close to breaking up two wonderful families through seductive lust.

This in no way excused Jim's behavior. He alone was responsible for his choices. She was angry with him and furious with the widow, yet she recognized that her actions and those of the widow might have influenced his choices. Though she may not have realized it at the time, this recognition was an important step in her later forgiveness of her husband. More important, she focused on saving her marriage and creating a healthy environment in which her children could grow up. She wanted her plan in place before there was any kind of confrontation.

Instead of wallowing in self-pity or guilt or playing the blame game, the wife viewed the situation clearly and prayed for guidance. Soon, the plan was clear in her mind. First, she eliminated some unnecessary community activities in which she had allowed herself to be involved. Second, she improved her wardrobe for the bedroom and took the initiative to plan some weekends away for the two of them. She could feel their closeness returning—their inner worlds retouching. Their family time with the children became more creative, and their worship time became more valuable.

On the few occasions thereafter when she suspected that her husband might be seeing the widow, she kissed him good-bye warmly and welcomed him home as if nothing had happened. Then, one Sunday after worship, he said with desperation in his voice, "Honey, we have to talk." She called their most trusted sitter, and she and her husband drove to a quiet meadow in the country where they often had gone to talk during their courtship period. Jim poured out news of the whole affair in a torrent of guilt and tears. She didn't interrupt, but let him get it all out as he begged her to forgive him. Very quietly, she replied, "I know, Jim; I have known intuitively for months, and I do forgive you." In amazement, he asked, "But how could you have done all the wonderful things you have done in the face of my betrayal? And how can you forgive me?"

She had prayed for this moment, so she knew exactly what to say: "It is the hardest thing I have ever had to do, but I didn't do it alone. My Christian faith held me steady, and my empowerment came from God through the Holy Spirit. Also, I was empowered by my love for you. I knew that your actions belied the man I had married."

They talked for hours, and at his request, they went back to the church where he asked for God's forgiveness. The only person in whom the wife had confided was her trusted pastor. He was the one who led them in a private ceremony to renew their marriage vows. He also told the wife that she had beaten the widow at her own game.

What a difference in the lives of two families. One woman reacted emotionally. The other stayed calm, thought clearly, and trusted God for guidance. Incidentally, the widow was later involved in a divorce suit from another wife. The divorce was so messy and costly that the widow left town in disgrace.

This story is not intended to be a blueprint for handling a marriage crisis, for every situation is different. The point here is that Jochebed's three tips for handling a crisis—remain calm, think clearly, and trust God—can be applied in *any* situation. Instead of allowing our emotions to rule us, we can choose to rule our emotions.

Lesson 3: We must learn to see the "big picture."

Often we tend to focus on one aspect of a given situation and make it the big issue. In Lesson 2, the big issue for each of the wives was not hurt pride, embarrassment, or even adultery—although each of these was an issue that had to be faced. The big issue was reconciliation—establishing an enduring marriage as well as a home where children could be lovingly nurtured by their parents.

In the situation of the first couple, the wife focused on her pride. Despite the fact that the incident had happened years earlier and during one of the many times when she had "run home to mother," this bitter wife saw herself only as a victim. The second wife, however, was able to look past her embarrassment and even the sin of adultery to focus on the "big picture." Hers was not a denial of the truth but an ability to stay focused on what she wanted to be accomplished in her marriage and her life.

Centuries earlier, Jochebed, a godly Hebrew woman, didn't just focus on one aspect of the situation: Pharaoh's dastardly action. Rather, she used her creative thought and energy on the "big picture": saving her baby.

Lesson 4: We may not live to see God's purposes fulfilled in our children, but we can trust God for the future.

In an uneasy time following two cancer surgeries and ten months of chemotherapy, I really didn't know what my future held; but I was certain Who held the future. In the same way, after we have done all we can to help our children be responsible and faithful, we must trust God for the future. We must trust the God who, as the apostle Paul said, "is able to do immeasurably more than all we can ask or imagine, according to his power that is at work within us" (Ephesians 3:20, NIV).

My guess is that Jochebed had no idea the baby she hid in a basket would be God's choice as deliverer for the Hebrew people. Though the Bible doesn't say when she died, it is unlikely that Jochebed lived long enough to see her three children involved in God's plan to confront the pharaoh and to lead the Hebrew people out of slavery, across the Red Sea, and through the wilderness en route to the Promised Land. After all, Moses was eighty years old when God spoke to him at the burning bush. What we do know is that her love for God and her faithfulness to God were steady, and she passed these spiritual qualities on to her three children.

Let us always be sensitive to the fact that our children and grandchildren may be "tapped" for one of God's grand designs. We have it within our power to enhance or obliterate this design. I believe that we obliterate, or at least delay, God's plan when we spiritually grow cold or cynical; when we destroy our children's self-confidence through criticism, neglect, or abuse; and when we are unaware of their need for role models. On the other hand, we can enhance God's plan by building a solid foundation in their lives so that God can have room to work easily. We can't build all the rooms in our children's houses of life—teachers, peers, circumstances—and their own wills influence these. But we can and must build strong foundations of unconditional love, encouragement, discipline (coming from the root word "to teach"), fun, education, and good role models of Christian living—which include regularly attending Sunday school and church, saying blessings at meals, having family devotions, and serving others. Enhancing God's design for our children, however, does not mean manipulating them to choose a church-related vocation. We plant the seeds, but God does the watering and gives the increase. Trust God on this one!

In our own family, we have watched in amazement as God has been mightily at work in the life of our oldest granddaughter. At age eighteen, she is a much stronger Christian than any of us were at that age. All we have done as grandparents is to help reinforce the strong foundation built by her parents. Though Ellen thoroughly enjoys all parts of being a teenager—athletics, academics, friendships, parties, and church—the moral decisions she has made could come only from a close relationship with Jesus Christ. We know that she will be strongly tested in her first year at college, but she will have lots of people back home loving and praying for her. We are trusting God for that.

In his book *The Prophet*, Kahil Gibran uses this analogy: Parents are bows and children are arrows. To parents he says, "Let your bending in the Archer's hand be for gladness. For even as he loves the arrow that flies, so He loves also the bow that is stable." If we can rejoice in God's love for us and our children, take time to enjoy our children, and trust God for the future, we will enhance God's plans for their lives. Jochebed certainly trusted God, and God proved to be trustworthy.

Digging a Little Deeper

1. Read Exodus 2:1-10. How do you know that Jochebed was a woman of character and wisdom? Discuss your thoughts.

2. Read Exodus 2:4-8. For what tasks had Jochebed well prepared her seven-year-old daughter? How might these responsibilities have helped prepare Miriam for some of the tasks she would face in helping her brothers take the Israelites through the wilderness?

3. Read Exodus 14:13-14. Even though Jochebed was able to have Moses with her only until he was weaned, evidently she was able to instill in him a faith in the one true God. When Moses spoke to the children of Israel as they stood at the Red Sea before the waters parted, what did he say that lets us know his mother's faith had become operative in his life?

4. Read Exodus 1:15-22 and 2:2-3. The Hebrew women of Egypt who were with child must have felt absolute panic upon hearing Pharaoh's horrible decree. How do we know that Jochebed stayed calm, thought clearly, and trusted God? What part of this plan would she have been unable to complete if she had been filled with fear and worry?

5. How do you tend to react when faced with a crisis? Describe a crisis you have experienced. Did you react emotionally, or calmly, like Jochebed? Why?

6. What is your reaction to the story of the two married women who reacted so differently to the crises in their marriages? What do you think you would do in a similar situation? What role would your Christian faith play in deciding your course of action?

7. Though the Bible story of Jochebed doesn't give a specific answer, what do you think enabled her to keep from focusing on only one aspect, Pharaoh's decree, and see the "big picture," which was saving her baby? Review Exodus 2:1-10.

8. Do you trust God enough to see beyond the hurt or bad news or fear in your life and see the "big picture" of what is most important to you? Give an example to illustrate your response.

9. What leads us to believe Jochebed didn't live to see the way in

which her children were used for the deliverance of the Hebrew people? How old do scholars believe Moses was when God called him from the burning bush? Read the story of the burning bush found in Exodus 3 and read Stephen's telling of Moses' story in Acts 7, especially verses 20 through 30.

10. What is our responsibility in preparing our children to fulfill God's purposes for their lives? Looking back on your own childhood and youth, how did your parents and/or other important adults in your life help prepare you for God's plan for your life?

5.

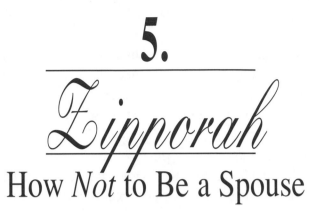

How *Not* to Be a Spouse

Scripture Text: **Exodus 2:5–4:26; 18:1-6**

Moses agreed to stay with the man [Jethro], and he gave Moses his daughter Zipporah in marriage.

—*Exodus 2:21*

Zipporah's Story

When Jochebed, Moses' mother, was allowed by Pharaoh's daughter to be his nursemaid, she had the opportunity to train her son well in his early years. Pharaoh's daughter, of course, had no idea that Jochebed was the child's mother. During those formative years, this godly Hebrew woman gave her son not only a love for the true God but also a deep sensitivity to the suffering of his people.

Years later, when Moses was a young man, he would leave the palace and walk among the Hebrews as they labored to make bricks for Pharaoh. With each visit, he was incensed that God's people had been enslaved and were being treated so badly. Each time he returned to the palace upset and angry.

One day, on a routine visit, Moses saw an Egyptian slave driver beating a Hebrew. Suddenly, his repressed and budding hostility flowered into rage, and he struck the Egyptian (Exodus 2:11-12).

Perhaps he didn't mean to kill the man; but realizing that he had, he hastily buried the body in the sand. Alas, word of the murder spread quickly, which Moses discovered the following day when he walked among the Hebrews and sought to resolve a dispute between two of the men. One responded, "Who made you a ruler and judge over us? Do you mean to kill me as you killed the Egyptian?" (Exodus 2:14). Knowing that he would be slain by Pharaoh for this deed, Moses fled the country.

As he was journeying into the land of Midian, Moses sat down to rest by a well. Imagine the surprise of the seven daughters of Jethro, the shepherd priest, when they encountered a well-dressed, cultured Egyptian who offered to help them water Jethro's flock. When the girls returned home and told about the handsome Egyptian, Jethro sent them back to Moses to offer him food and lodging. Now a refugee from his homeland, Moses gratefully accepted the offer. There he remained and became a shepherd for Jethro, the kind Midianite.

The Bible doesn't say exactly how it happened, so join me in creating a "scene." Jethro had seven daughters, and all of them were eager to get married. None of the "local boys" had the charm, culture, or good looks of the Egyptian. Moses was the catch of the century! The race was on, with each girl finding subtle ways to get his attention. Moses was away from home and lonely—a common reason many men and women have made unwise decisions when choosing a mate.

Why did Moses choose Zipporah? No one knows for sure, but consider this: Moses had been surrounded by beautiful, glamorous women in Pharaoh's palace. I can imagine that he chose the most attractive of the seven readily available daughters. Unfortunately, she also was self-centered, ill-tempered, and neurotic (Exodus 4:25). In other words, she was an inadequate wife. In addition, there is nothing in Scripture indicating that she ever believed in God.

The strongest evidence of Zipporah's ill-tempered nature came when Moses, Zipporah, and their two sons were going toward Egypt to carry out the biggest mandate of Moses' life—to ask Pharaoh to free the Hebrews. If ever a man needed a balanced, caring wife, it was Moses as he undertook that great endeavor. He was unsure about whether he could do what God was asking, and he was fearful of facing Pharaoh again. But instead of supporting her husband, Zipporah was neurotic and confrontational.

You see, as an unbeliever, she refused to allow their youngest son, Eliezer, to be circumcised (Joan Comay, *Who's Who in the Old Testament*, Nashville: Festival Books, Abingdon Press, 1971, pp. 490, 659), even though she knew that circumcision was a sacred ritual to an Israelite—circumcision represented a part of the Israelite covenant with God. In order to keep peace in the family, Moses did not force the issue; but he must have felt guilty whenever he thought of it. When Moses became seriously ill on the way to Egypt and Zipporah thought he was going to die, she was sure that God was punishing him because their son was not circumcised. Then, not out of faith but out of fear—fear that she would be left alone with two small children in a strange land—Zipporah grabbed a sharp stone and cut off their son's foreskin, leaving the child screaming in pain. Hysterically, she picked up the bloody foreskin and rubbed it on her husband's foot, saying, "You are a bridegroom of blood to me!" (Exodus 4:25). Moses knew he didn't have the strength to fulfill God's command and deal with his wife's neurotic behavior simultaneously, so he must have sent Zipporah and the children back to the safety of her father's home (Exodus 18:2-3).

When Moses was well again, God sent Aaron, and later Miriam, to accompany him and assist in the gigantic undertaking (Exodus 4:27-31). The Bible doesn't mention Zipporah again until we read that Jethro brought her and the two sons to visit Moses after the Israelites had crossed the Red Sea and were living in the wilderness (Exodus 18:5-8).

In the Scriptures, there is no mention of Moses and Zipporah ever seeing each other again. I have often thought that if Moses had lived after Christ came, he would have had "light" enough to have helped Zipporah change. Instead, his life of faith was lived in the "twilight zone" between darkness and light, so he probably did the very best he knew how to do. When we live in "darkness" as Zipporah did—whether it's because of unbelief or simply a choice to live by secular values—we can never be totally adequate in our own strength. Unfortunately, Zipporah's inadequacies caused an irreparable rift in her marriage. The good news for us, however, is that we can learn from her example.

What Can We Learn From Zipporah?

Lesson 1: God should be at the center of the marriage relationship.

You might say that the marriage of Moses and Zipporah was destined for trouble from the start, for they did not share a common belief in the one true God. Yet even the most committed Christians today—who have the advantage not only of knowing God's complete plan of redemption through Jesus Christ but also of knowing and walking in fellowship with Christ himself—still find that marriage is hard. Part of the reason for the difficulty is our own wavering faith commitment; another part is the secular culture of our day, which even imperceptibly influences our behavior; and another part is the timeless truth that living in such a close relationship brings out the quirks in our personalities and behaviors, which sometimes surprise even us. Even so, I am convinced that the closest we come to heaven or hell on earth is the experience of marriage. The good news is that a happy marriage doesn't just happen by chance. With the help of Christ, we can *build* happy marriages—but not overnight.

Except for the faith you live by, there is no decision more important than the choice of the one with whom you will share your life in marriage. It affects every aspect of living. For that reason, we should never marry for the wrong reasons: loneliness, physical attraction only, social status or wealth, and so forth. Nor should we marry a person whose core values are extremely different from our own. This is why Paul says that a Christian should not marry a nonbeliever (2 Corinthians 6:14). Such a union is like a carriage with two horses pulling in different directions, or a river with cross currents—as a result, the children are caught in the cross currents. A Christian home cannot be established unless Christ is at the center of the home.

Since husbands and wives come from different backgrounds, each brings a different set of expectations about a multitude of things. This is especially evident in child-rearing practices. Keeping Christ at the center of the home may mean one thing for the husband and another for the wife. My husband and I decided that the best way we could keep Christ in the center of our home was to stay as close as possible to Christ in our individual lives—"practicing the presence" through personal devotions, prayer, corporate worship, and commitment. Of course, this approach must be mixed with lots of love, laughter, flexibility, and the ability to see the other person's point of view. Even then, we will never get it exactly right; but if we are committed to making Christ central, we will grow in our ability to do so.

Recently, I was talking with a physician from India whose marriage was arranged by his parents. He had never seen his wife until their wedding day, yet they have been happily married for twenty-five years. When I pointed out that the custom of pre-arranged marriages seems strange to our culture, he reminded me that many if not most Americans get married because of physical attraction only. The Indian parents consider similarities in personality and background, such as temperament, family values, faith, and education. He also noted that the divorce rate in India is much lower than in America.

I'm certainly not advocating prearranged marriages, but there is a lesson here. Common values, priorities, and interests are the "glue" that holds marriages together; and for Christians, the most important ingredient of that "glue" is a strong relationship with Jesus Christ. Regardless of the difficulties a Christian couple may have, if they will continually work to keep Christ in the center of their relationship and home life, then they will be on their way to a loving and lasting marriage.

Lesson 2: Self-centeredness is one of the biggest obstacles to a happy marriage.

Zipporah is "exhibit A" for the destructive effect self-centeredness can have in a marriage. Most marriage counselors agree that the biggest obstacle to marital happiness is not unfaithfulness, sexual problems, money, or in-laws; rather, it is consistent self-centeredness on the part of one or both spouses. Self-centeredness is an unwillingness to see your partner's point of view, to understand his or her feelings, or to compromise.

I think of Debbie, an attractive and talented young woman who was full of anger and resentment. She and Chip had been married less than a year, and already she was sitting in my office for the third time, seeking advice. In fairness, I believe Debbie really wanted a happy marriage—but so did Zipporah. To each of them, happiness meant "doing it my way." In Debbie's case, she had grown up in a Christian home and was extremely active in her church. In fact, this is one of the things that was so appealing to Chip when he met her. Debbie, however, had learned to camouflage her selfishness with a million-dollar smile, a ready wit, and a natural ability to lead. She could manipulate a group into doing what she wanted and make them feel good about their decision. Yet in an intimate, one-on-one relationship, her motives were painfully obvious.

The previous two times she had come to my office, the problems had been minor. She simply was not getting her way, and she was behaving like a spoiled child. "He's simply not sensitive to my feelings," she had explained. Yet after examining the pattern of their marriage, she had seen how often Chip had proven his sensitivity to her feelings and requests and how often he actually had sacrificed for their relationship. Each time she had left the office willing to say, "I'm sorry" about her temper tantrums—something hard for her to do—and to make a minor adjustment.

This time, it was different. Chip's company had offered him a promotion, but it would mean a move to another city. Before they were married, Chip had outlined the possibility of such a move, explaining that when you turn down a promotion without reason, the company usually left you in the same position forever. At the time, Debbie had seen no problem with a potential move. After all, she was gregarious and ambitious, and a new opportunity would be a challenge.

Now she was refusing to go. It wasn't that she was settled into her chosen career. Actually, she was working in an incidental job, but she liked the job and felt that it showcased her talents to the community. By her own admission, however, she would have given up the job in a heartbeat if a better offer had come along.

"Debbie, you are so outgoing and talented, you can find another job in the new city—probably a better one since the city is larger," I suggested. She agreed, adding that she knew the promotion would be good for their financial future. "Then, what's the problem?" I asked. With anger spewing from her words, she said, "I don't want Chip to win again." Egotism and selfishness were starkly evident in her motive. Very calmly I asked, "But Debbie, didn't you promise that you would cooperate if a promotion should come?"

Her anger suddenly turned on me. "Wait a minute," she said.

"Whose side are you on?" Swiftly but softly I responded, "On the side of a happy marriage for you and Chip."

"I'm not going to be a doormat. I don't even believe *God* expects that!" she nearly screamed. "Neither do I," I said. "I believe that God sees each of us as persons of great worth—not because of what we have accomplished, but because of what he did for us through Christ. But God expects us to act like adults in adult situations, not like children. When we are committed to another person in marriage, God expects us to make decisions for the total good—not for our own interests."

In frustration, she picked up her coat to leave, saying, "You just don't understand." As she stood at the door, I said as firmly and lovingly as I could, "Debbie, you are at a crossroads in your marriage, but the fight is not between you and Chip. It's between your ego and Christ. Who will be Lord in your life? Only you can decide."

As she walked out of my office, I thought sadly that she was walking away from her marriage. It was sometime later that I walked down the hall. Faintly at first, then more loudly, I heard sobs coming from the sanctuary. Quietly, I slipped into a pew and prayed for the beautiful young woman who was in the midst of the fight of her life. It was quite some time before the sobs ceased. When she arose, she saw me. She walked toward me, smiling. As she hugged me tightly, she said, "I have just taken a quantum leap toward spiritual and emotional maturity—thanks to you." I replied, "No, not thanks to me, but thanks to Christ and to your willingness to hear him." Debbie nodded as she walked home to pack.

That experience happened years ago. Thankfully, there was a happy ending for Chip and Debbie. Yet for Zipporah and Moses, there was no happy ending. From what the Scriptures tell us, they saw each other only once after the Hebrews left Egypt. Today, in a culture in which radical individualism is often lauded as having ultimate value, the difference between individual worth and self-centeredness is blurred. "Me-ism" denies the importance of home, school, church, and community life; and it raises personal pleasure to the highest social level. Individual worth, on the other hand, proclaims that we are worthy because we are created and loved by God, redeemed by Christ, and empowered by the Holy Spirit. Self-centeredness (I want what I want when I want it) cannot work in relationships—especially the close relationship of marriage. In addition to loving each other as husband and wife, we must be respectful, flexible, willing to compromise, forgiving, and willing to work together as a team.

Lesson 3: When two individuals come together in marriage, adjustments and disagreements are to be expected—and handled with love and care.

I agree totally with Ruth Bell Graham, who is reported to have said, "When two people agree all the time on everything, one of them is unnecessary." As separate and unique individuals, it's simply impossible—and undesirable—for married couples to avoid disagreements 100 percent of the time. The problem is not that we disagree, but that often we do so in a destructive way.

One of the things I learned early in marriage is that disagreements should be about issues, not about "tearing down" the other person. That's why it is so important for us to avoid saying things in anger that will be painfully remembered for years to come. Consider Moses and Zipporah. Moses' relationship to God and the rituals of his faith were sacred to him. Zipporah not only refused to allow their son to be circumcised, but she also blamed Moses' illness on his God. Then, after circumcising their son herself, she rubbed Moses' foot with the bloody foreskin and said these hurtful words: "Truly you are a bridegroom of blood to me!" (Exodus 4:25). It hurt so deeply that their marriage was never the same again. Realizing that she could never participate willingly in God's great design, Moses sent her home with their two sons; and as far as we know, they saw each other only one time after that painful incident.

Perhaps Moses and Zipporah's example is a bit extreme, but the principle applies to every disagreement between husband and wife: Instead of intentionally trying to hurt or "tear down" our spouse with our words and actions, we should try to protect our spouse's feelings and even build him or her up by being loving, considerate, and gentle. The key is to recognize our spouse's "Achilles heels"—those sensitive areas that cause her or him pain or embarrassment—and avoid those areas in our disagreements. It could be a weight problem, sensitivity to criticism, family background, lack of education, a past mistake or hurt, a specific fear, or many other things. We never should "attack" our spouse at vulnerable points, no matter how upset we are. If we are consistently loving, caring, and encouraging to our mate, then our disagreements can be objective and even helpful to our relationship by forcing us out of narrow thinking and enabling us to see the issues from another point of view.

Digging a Little Deeper

1. Read 2 Corinthians 6:14-17. Why do you think the apostle Paul was so adamant in saying that believers should not be yoked with nonbelievers? What difficulties or challenges are involved in an "unequally yoked" marriage?
2. In the culture of Old Testament days, the oldest daughter generally was the first given in marriage. Read Genesis 29:16-30, which tells how Jacob wanted to marry Rebekah but was given Leah instead. Now read Exodus 2:16-21. Is there anything in these verses that indicates a similar situation might have occurred with Moses and Zipporah? Think carefully about their marriage. Why do you think they chose each other?

3. What do you think are the important things to consider when you are choosing a marriage partner? Why?

4. Read Exodus 4:18-26. What effect did Zipporah's selfish and neurotic behavior have on her marriage?

5. What is the difference between radical individualism ("me-ism") and the Christian belief in the worth of the individual? How can each belief affect a marriage relationship?

6. Do you believe that a husband and wife should agree about everything? Why? Why is it important not to attack your spouse's "Achilles' heel" or vulnerable point during a disagreement?

7. Why was the circumcision of his son so important to Moses, a Hebrew man? Why do you think Zipporah refused to allow their second son to be circumcised (Exodus 4:18-26)?

8. What are some of the things you most appreciate in your mate? Are you as liberal with your affirmation and encouragement as with your criticism?

6.

The Original "Career Woman"

Scripture Text: Exodus 2:1-11; 15:20-21; Numbers 12; 20:1; Micah 6:4

For I brought you up from the land of Egypt,
and redeemed you from the house of slavery;
and I sent before you Moses, Aaron, and Miriam.

—Micah 6:4

Miriam's Story

Even as a little girl, Miriam was self-reliant and responsible. Her mother, Jochebed, had taught her oldest child well. She was the seven-year-old who waited quietly in the bulrushes, watching her baby brother, Moses, until the pharaoh's daughter discovered him. It was she who asked the princess if she would like to have a Hebrew nurse. When the answer was, "Yes, go," Miriam ran to get her mother and took her to the princess. She neither giggled nor gave any other expression that might cast suspicion on Jochebed's true identity (Exodus 2:3-10).

At that early age, Miriam was becoming a patriot. She believed, as her parents did, in the true God and in his promise to make of the Hebrews a great nation. The Bible doesn't tell us what she was doing during the years of waiting—the years when Moses was living in the palace and later in Midian. I believe she was ministering to her people in their enslaved suffering—helping them to trust in God's deliverance, counseling and encouraging them. It is clear that they loved her, for when she became ill in the wilderness years later, they would not move on without her (Numbers 12:15).

Neither does the Bible tell us why Miriam never married. In Hebrew culture, a woman's highest achievement was to be married and to have children, particularly sons. There is no indication that she turned down suitors. My guess is that Miriam was so caught up in the cause of building a great Hebrew nation that she had neither the time, interest, nor energy to be domestic. She was a nationalist.

In today's terms, you might say that Miriam was the first woman to "break the glass ceiling." She was the original career woman. Her leadership qualities were everywhere evident. Though Moses and Aaron had the logistical task of moving two million people across the Red Sea and through the wilderness, Miriam is the one who put spirit into the people. In fact, when they were safely across the Red Sea, she grabbed her tambourine and led them in singing the first national anthem: "Sing ye to the LORD, for he hath triumphed gloriously: / the horse and his rider hath he thrown into the sea" (Exodus 15:21, KJV).

Charles Wesley, who, with his brother John, began the Methodist movement in England, is reported to have said that a great idea becomes a movement when there is commitment on the part of the people and enthusiastic singing. Miriam needed to help the Israelites sing joyfully. After all, they had had great uncertainty about whether they could get across the Red Sea. They also were afraid of Pharaoh and what punishment he would inflict upon them if they were made to return to Egypt. And they were not sure what they would face before they reached the

Promised Land. Miriam must have known that singing enthusiastically and remembering God's presence with them would bring hope and courage for the future. There is no indication that she was good at strategic planning—Moses and Aaron did that—but she, more than the other two, gave spirit to the Israelites.

Unfortunately, a dark blot appeared on the otherwise incredible achievements of this prophetess, poet, and leader of the Hebrew nation. In a word, it was jealousy. She was angered when Moses married again—jealous of the woman's influence on her illustrious brother. Most scholars agree that Zipporah had long since died when Moses married a second time, but even if she had not, there was nothing in their culture at that time that forbade a man to have another wife.

I am sure that one reason Miriam didn't approve of the marriage was that the woman was not a Hebrew. She was an Ethiopian from Cush. Miriam also may have reasoned that since she herself had been willing to forgo marriage, remain celibate, and give all her energies to building the new nation, Moses should have done so as well. Whatever she may have thought, Miriam led a nasty campaign against her brother and convinced Aaron, the high priest, to join the group. Her greatest offense was her sarcastic rejection of the leadership of Moses. She had been a symbol of unity in the nation, but she became the divisive leader of discord. Miriam and Aaron said to the people: "Has the LORD spoken only through Moses? Has he not spoken through us also?" (Numbers 12:2). Is it possible that she wanted to establish joint partnership with her brother Aaron, in state power, and eliminate the power of Moses? I also have wondered if, because she was an aging woman, she resented the fact that a younger and more beautiful woman was so influential in the life of Moses.

Whatever the reason, the discord became so bad that God came to settle the conflict. God summoned the three of them to come to the Tabernacle. In no uncertain terms, God reprimanded Miriam and Aaron for hurting Moses and failing in their duties to God. Moses received vindication as God's faithful servant; because never once did Moses respond to the insults directed at him. Then, as the divine cloud lifted from the Tabernacle, Aaron turned to his sister and was aghast to see that she was leprous (Numbers 12:10). Both brothers were overcome with love for their sister and prayed that her punishment be removed from her. God heard their prayers and decreed that she live outside the camp for only seven days before she was healed. As I've mentioned previously, the fact that the Israelite people did not go on until she was able to join them indicates her great influence (Numbers 12:15-16).

Though we don't know exactly when Miriam died, we do know that it was before they reached the Promised Land. In the book *Bible Characters* (Zondervan Publishing House, Grand Rapids, 1952), Alexander Whyte suggests that Miriam died soon after her terrible week of leprosy—and that she died not of old age but of a broken heart. She was buried at Kadesh-Barnea, where for thirty days the Israelites mourned her passing. Miriam dedicated her life to the Hebrew people, and she is remembered along with Moses and Aaron as the leaders of the Exodus.

What Can We Learn From Miriam?

Lesson 1: Whether married or single, a woman can have a meaningful and fulfilling life if she has a dream that gives her life purpose.

Even today when more women are part of the work force than ever before in the history of our nation, many women believe that they are "incomplete" or "deficient" in some way unless they are married. The truth is that a woman's life is not defined by marriage or family position. She is never just an extension of someone else. In God's sight, one is a "whole number."

Miriam knew this truth. She knew that a God-given dream is what gives a life meaning and purpose. Her God-given dream was the creation of a new nation. And as she pursued this dream, her leadership skills and creativity blossomed in multiple accomplishments—making her not only a visionary leader but also a prophetess, poet, and musician.

In addition to Miriam, countless single women have followed their dreams and have contributed to the betterment of our world beyond measure. Joan of Arc was a bold and committed Christian who led a French Resistance Army to get the Dauphin crowned in Rheims Cathedral in 1430. Florence Nightingale, the daughter of wealthy English parents, left her good life and, in 1854, became the first nurse to serve in the Crimean War. American Susan B. Anthony helped establish the National American Suffrage Association in 1869. Mother Teresa, a nun of Calcutta, India, began in 1950 to establish homes throughout India where the homeless could find love and care and, as necessary, a place to die in dignity.

Likewise, married women through the ages have improved the world through their efforts, perhaps beginning with Deborah of the Old Testament—a judge, prophetess, and military leader in the twelfth century B.C. (Judges 4:4-10).

Four married women from the United States also deserve special mention. The first is Barbara Heck (1734–1804). Barbara and her husband, Paul, came from Ireland to the new world and settled in New York. She is known as the Mother of Methodism because she organized the first Methodist congregation in America. The congregation grew rapidly, and today the John Street Methodist Church in New York's busy financial district stands on the very spot of her first church. There is a plaque on the church carrying the names of Barbara R. Heck and the church's first pastor, Philip Embury.

The second is Ann Judson (1789–1826), who was the first

American woman missionary to the Far East. Married to Adoniram Judson, Ann suffered with her husband in his pioneering experiences in Burma and saved his life during the war between the English and Burmese in 1824–1826. She assisted him in his translation of the Bible into Burmese and wrote a history of the Burma Mission.

The third is Mary Bethune (1875–1955), who was married to Albertus Bethune. She studied at Moody Bible Institute, became an educator, and founded the Daytona Normal and Industrial Institute for Negro Girls. Later, she was an effective Civil Rights leader and a member of the National Association for Colored Women.

The fourth is Lillian Gilbreth (1878–1972), who was married to Frank Gilbreth. She was recognized as the foremost woman engineer and efficiency expert in her time. Lillian, a graduate of the University of California and Brown University, used psychology, management, and scientific methods to discover a way to make jobs more productive.

Whether married or single, all these diverse women have one thing in common: a dream. A God-given dream is perhaps the most motivating and empowering force known to humankind!

Lesson 2: Those who encourage others can change the world!

Miriam had the wonderful gift of encouragement. It has been said that the word *encourage* means "to put heart into someone" and the word *discourage* means "to take heart out of someone." Miriam put heart into the Hebrew people during the Exodus from Egypt. She gave them hope when the going was hard, and she put a song in their hearts. And I believe that they couldn't have lived in the wilderness so long if they hadn't been able to sing!

I have a friend who is like Miriam. She seems to have ESP (Extra Spiritual Perception). If I am ever feeling down a bit, I know that I will receive a call from her. She receives and responds to God's nudges. When I see her or hear her voice on the tele-phone, something "singing" happens within me. She has the abil-ity to help you believe in yourself—to really believe Philippians 4:13: "I can do all things through [Christ] who strengthens me." She is one of the most positive, faith-filled, fun persons I have ever met. As a result, everyone who comes into contact with her walks straighter—and several feet taller. What a gift!

As Christians, all of us should be encouragers. Our primary spiritual gift may not be encouragement, but if we follow the example and teachings of Jesus, we will lift others up. We can do this in simple ways such as smiling, being aware of and sensitive to the needs of others, showing respect to all persons, offering the gift of friendship, including people in group conversation, and laughing with others—as well as offering the "bigger gifts of hos-pitality." These "bigger gifts" include such things as making our homes, our businesses, our churches, and our organizations places of hospitality; and expressing in tangible ways love and concern for others.

Lesson 3: Though we must strive to "run the race" of life with integrity and honor, we cannot win the "prize" by our own efforts but only by the grace of God.

The Bible gives an honest evaluation of its characters, high-lighting their strengths and never downplaying their weaknesses. It's sad when a weakness comes at the end of an illustrious career, such as in Miriam's life, because people often remember the weakness more than the person's strengths. Fortunately for Miriam, the fact that the grace of God was mediated quickly and lovingly through her brothers—especially Moses—helps us remember her strengths. By eliminating any conflict among the three of them through forgiveness, Moses and Aaron prepared the way for God's grace to flow freely to the sister whom they both loved.

As a result of forgiveness and grace, Miriam's sin of jealousy is rarely mentioned; rather, she is remembered for her strengths, her belief in and devotion to the one true God, her investment in the dream of a new nation, and her courage to work a lifetime to help achieve that dream. She was an encourager, a prophetess, a poet, and a musician. All of these gifts she used joyfully in service to God.

The humbling incident in Miriam's life recorded in Numbers 12 also underscores a vital truth: We must "press on toward the goal for the prize of the heavenly call of God in Christ Jesus" (Philippians 3:14); and we win that prize, not by our own efforts, but by the grace of God. There's a popular saying: "Christians aren't perfect, only forgiven." Indeed, none of us is perfect; we all make mistakes and sin somewhere along the course of life. Yet God's grace is sufficient for us (2 Corinthians 12:9).

In a town where I once lived, there was a man who was "Mr. Everything." He was president of our largest bank, president of the Chamber of Commerce, chairman of the board of his church, and a genuinely fine human being. He was generous and helped many people save their homes and businesses. He had a large house, a place at the lake, several cars, a beautiful wife, and two beautiful daughters. In the eyes of most people, he had achieved the American dream.

One day, this man rocked our community when he left town with another woman. To his credit, he left behind all his financial resources for his wife and daughters. Even so, the community sided with his family. For years and years, "Mr. Everything" had run the race of life with integrity and honor; then, tragically, he got off course. He made a major mistake, and all the good of his lifetime was wiped out in the memory of townspeople by that one act.

Despite the "detour" this man chose to take, the pain and grief he caused others, and the community's low opinion of him, there still is a possibility that he finished the race victoriously. You see, our loving, forgiving God is willing to restore each of us, if only we will seek his forgiveness and accept his grace. I'll never know how the "race" ended for "Mr. Everything," but I do know this: It's never too late to get back on course, with God's help, and win the race with integrity and honor.

Lesson 4: Pride leads to egotism and jealousy, which can destroy us.

Miriam's life points out two destructive temptations that stem from the same source: pride. First, there is the temptation to think more highly of ourselves and our abilities than we should. When we allow our egos to become inflated, when we lose our humility, we often find ourselves striving to be in control, to "run things"—especially those with strong leadership skills. Perhaps we see what is happening around us and feel we could do it better. Or perhaps we simply don't like the way things are going and want to have it our way. Only submission to Christ as our Lord— in addition to our Savior and Friend—can save us from our own self-centered egos or wills. Through the Holy Spirit, Christ enables us not only to cooperate with and help those whose skills may not be as strong as our own, but also to submit our wills to the will of God—and to do so *joyfully*.

The second destructive temptation that stems from pride is "the green-eyed monster": jealousy. This "monster" is quick to consume us and destroy our peace. There is a legend about some followers of Satan who tried to tempt a holy man with women and wine and an elegant home. Nothing disturbed his equanimity. Seeing their efforts, Satan said, "Your methods are too obvious. Allow me." After asking only one question of the man, a scowl replaced the holy man's peaceful countenance and he soon lost his cool. The question Satan asked was this: "Did you know that your brother has just been elected Bishop of Alexandria?" The tool Satan used was jealousy.

According to psychiatrists, jealousy is the backwash of personal insecurity. It often comes from a "greedy" eagerness to have the recognition and approval of others. Generally speaking, we are jealous of those peers or rivals who have outdistanced us a bit. For example, an actress in a community theater is not jealous of Meryl Streep or Angela Lansbury; instead, she is jealous of a local woman who got the part in the play that she wanted for herself. It is not surprising, then, that jealousy usually occurs among people of the same profession, career, or "station" in life. For example, ministers are jealous not of doctors, but of other ministers; a young married couple is jealous not of their retired next-door neighbors, but the prospering young couple down the street.

Only the Great Physician can heal us from the sin of pride and its accompanying temptations of egotism and jealousy, and the "prescription" is this: Seek to "have the mind of Christ" (1 Corinthians 2:16). In his Letter to the Philippians, Paul expressed it this way: "Let the same mind be in you that was in Christ Jesus" (2:5). To get a better idea of what this means, let us consider how Christ protected himself against the "shafts of jealousy" that were aimed at him by the Pharisees and the Sanhedrin:

- He didn't compare himself with others. If ever we conclude that we are better or more able than others, we are trapped by the sin of pride.
- He viewed jealousy as a sickness of the soul—a sin of the spirit. We should never ignore jealousy when it rears its ugly head at us. Instead, we should follow the example of Christ when he was tempted regarding the way he would live and conduct his ministry. He spent more time in prayer so that he might be led by God's spirit (Luke 4:1-12).
- Jesus knew that God has a plan, and that God has given each believer a spiritual gift to help accomplish that plan. We each must seek our gift and use it for God's glory. Remember that

when Peter was unduly concerned about the destiny of John and asked, "Lord, what about him?" Jesus replied, "What is that to you? Follow me!" (John 21:21-22).

• He lived independently of praise, and he can take away our greedy eagerness for human praise and adulation.

• He never provoked jealousy in others, and he can teach us to wear our success with humility—especially with old friends. We must learn to emphasize old equalities rather than new differences.

In our culture, we are encouraged to be prideful. One day on the front page of our local paper appeared a large picture of our "winningest" football team. All the players were holding up their forefingers, and the headline read, "We Are Number One!" As Christians, although we should feel confident because of Christ's power within us, we should remain humble because Christ is the source of our power.

In contrast to the football team, consider a man from India who has retired as the Indian Ambassador to Peru and who previously was ambassador to Mexico. My husband and I heard him speak recently. He was erudite, sophisticated, and affable. But he also demonstrated great humility, as well as respect for all people. We were not surprised to learn that he is a Christian.

When we give in to pride, we soon begin to "think of [ourselves] more highly than [we] ought to think" (Romans 12:3) and are tempted to be egotistical and controlling. But when we willingly choose humility, we discover the truth of this blessed paradox: "All who exalt themselves will be humbled, and all who humble themselves will be exalted" (Matthew 23:12).

Digging a Little Deeper

1. Read Jeremiah 29:11. This verse suggests that God's plans for us, individually and collectively, are for our good as well as for

the common good. Do you believe this to be true? Why or why not? Respond to this statement: We were created not to drift through life, but to be productive and make a difference for good and for God.

2. Read the following:

As a junior high school student, I suffered from a poor self-image because I was comparing myself with my sister, a very high achiever. My father told me that everyone was unique and had special talents and gifts. He added: "God put a treasure in you. It is different from your sister's or your brother's, and what your mother and I want to do is help you discover your treasure." He set me free to be me!

Have you discovered your "treasure" so that you can fit into God's plan? If you are in a group, share your responses with one another; then take turns telling one "treasure" you see in each person present. If alone, make a point this week to ask three people who know you well to identify the "treasure" they see in you. Often other people can see our "treasures" or gifts more readily than we can. Pray for God's guidance in discovering your treasure, and don't be surprised if God uses a friend of yours to point out some which you have overlooked.

3. Why is it important for us to encourage—or put heart into—others? In what ways do you do this?

4. What about our own need for encouragement? Where should we look for our encouragement? Read 1 Samuel 30:6. Where did David find his encouragement?

5. When have you felt distressed yet received strength and encouragement from God? Write about that experience in your journal if you are alone; discuss it if you are in a group.

6. Why do you think it was important for Miriam to lead the Israelites in singing after they had crossed the Red Sea (Exodus 15:21)?

7. The quotation "Christians aren't perfect, only forgiven" helps us know that the church is not a museum for saints, but a hospital for sinners. Since we are the church—or "the body of Christ," as Paul calls Christians—what does this call us to remember?

8. Read Matthew 7:1; Galatians 6:2; 1 Corinthians 12:27; and John 13:34-35. In what areas listed in these Scriptures do you need most improvement? Discuss.

9. Read 2 Corinthians 12:9. Do you believe, with Paul, that God's grace is sufficient for whatever circumstances we face? If so, why do you think we try to do it on our own—and often worry so much? Discuss.

10. Read Philippians 2:5. Paul suggests that when we have the same mind as Christ Jesus, we have taken a giant step toward getting rid of self-centered egotism. How do you cultivate or develop the thought patterns of Jesus in your own mind? Discuss.

11. When have you been guilty of one or both of pride's satellite sins: egotism and jealousy? What happened? How do you fight these sins in your life? What else can you do to be free of their grip?

12. Paul said that God has given each one of us at least one spiritual gift. Read the lists of gifts found in Romans 12:6-8; 1 Corinthians 12:4-11, 28; and Ephesians 4:11. What do you think is your one or primary gift, and how are you using it to glorify God?

7.

Prostitute Turned Believer

Scripture Text: Joshua 2:1-24; 6:1-25

"I know that the LORD has given you the land, and that dread of you has fallen on us."

—*Joshua 2:9*

Rahab's Story

The story of Rahab would make a terrific television drama. It has all the necessary ingredients: a beautiful leading lady with an independent spirit, a troubled past, and a life of wrong choices and pain; spies; a fearful king willing to stop at nothing to protect his kingdom; secrecy and danger; courage and bravery; a sacred oath; an exciting escape; intrigue; mystery; war; victory and defeat; and best of all, a happy ending. Join me as I combine biblical storytelling with some creative imagining. Our story begins at the point of the biblical story in Joshua 2:1, with the two spies spending the night at Rahab's house. Then we depart from the biblical story briefly to fill in some of the "holes" in Rahab's life. Because her early years are not recorded in the Scriptures, I have taken the liberty of creating a possible scenario of her life from youth until the time when her prostitution began. The biblical story picks up again when she hides the spies on her rooftop.

"Why do I trust these men from Gilgal?" Rahab wondered as she stretched out in bed. This was one of those rare nights when she was alone between the sheets. She had planned it that way so that she could sort out some of the events of recent days. Why was she acting so irrationally? Why had she hidden the two Hebrew spies, Caleb and Salmon*? What had caused her to lie about their whereabouts? If the king discovered the news, she would be killed immediately for treason.

Before she figured out what was going on in her mind to allow such action, she found herself reviewing her life. She knew she was the most beautiful woman in Jericho—although the past three years had taken their toll on her appearance as well as her perception of herself. As a teenager, she had been pretty and popular, and she had had an independent spirit. Her parents' rules had been much too restrictive; so when the innkeeper and his wife had offered her a job as a waitress, she had jumped at the chance. The job also had provided a room for her. When the owner had suggested she could buy the inn when she could afford it, she had begun saving every penny she could. Alas, they had paid her so little that it would take years to get even a down payment. She had been so discouraged that she almost had given in to her parents' pleas to return home—that is, until a tall, handsome man from the East, traveling with a caravan, had stopped at the inn.

As she had served the stranger dinner, she had asked questions about his country, and she had been fascinated with his description of a very different lifestyle. By the time she had served his coffee, he had made the suggestion that they spend the night together in his room. Shocked at the suggestion, she had adamantly refused until he told her the price he was willing to pay

* *Young's Analytical Concordance to the Bible* lists this spy Caleb as the grandson of Ephrath. Salmon is listed as husband to Rahab in Matthew 1:5, lending credence to him being the other spy. Also see *The Women of the Bible*, Herbert Lockyer, Zondervan, 1967; pp. 130–31, 133.

That was more money than she could make in months. Buying the inn might become a possibility after all. So her life of prostitution had begun.

What she hadn't counted on was the social ostracism she would experience when the community learned of her new profession; the deep disappointment and sadness of her parents; and the anger of the innkeepers, who had decided to leave the inn and had demanded that she buy it immediately. They had raised the price of the down payment to an almost impossible sum. But her business had become so good that she had been able to pay almost the entire amount within a year. To do so, she had steeled her heart against the ugly comments of people who once had been her friends. She often would toss her shiny, chestnut brown hair in a "who cares?" manner. In her heart, however, she felt lonely and unclean.

From some of the travelers, she had heard the story of the Hebrews and how God had parted the waters of the Red Sea so they could escape slavery in Egypt. For some strange and unfathomable reason, she began to believe in this God, though she knew little about him. When her heart was heavy, she thought of the power of that God, and somehow the pain in her heart was eased.

Recently, there had been rumors that the Israelites were planning to destroy the city of Jericho as they had Og and Sihon. Even strong men in Jericho were frightened. They didn't know what to expect or when to expect it. So, when the strange men appeared, asking for a place to stay, she knew they were Israelites because of their accents and clothes. Suddenly, as she looked into their fear-filled eyes, she also knew that they were spies. Perceiving this situation and knowing that she was taking a huge risk, Rahab took them to her rooftop and hid them under the flax she was drying. She knew that, out of fear of the Israelites and their powerful God, the king of Jericho was scrutinizing any new person who walked through the city gates. She was sure that

Caleb and Salmon had been spotted, and that soon the king's men would be standing at her door.

It happened exactly as she imagined. She scarcely had hidden the men before the pursuers stood at her front door, asking her to send the spies out. "The men were here," she said, "but they left quickly—before the city gates closed. You are welcome to search my house, but I am sure that if you leave immediately, you can overtake them." The men followed her advice.

Rahab went to the rooftop and told the spies what had happened. Then she said, "I know that the Lord has given you this land, and that a great fear of you has fallen upon us. . . . Now please swear to me by the Lord that you will show kindness to me because of my kindness to you. Give me a sure sign that you will spare the lives of my father and mother, my brothers and sisters, and all who belong to them, that you will save us from death" (Joshua 2:9-13, author's paraphrase).

"Our lives for your lives!" the men said to her. "If you don't tell what we are doing, we will treat you kindly and faithfully when the Lord gives us the land" (Joshua 2:14, author's paraphrase). Rahab let the men down by rope. Since her house was on top of the city wall, they would be outside the gate. She told them to go to the hills so that their pursuers would not find them. Then, after three days, the pursuers would return, and Caleb and Salmon could go back to the camp at Gilgal.

"But remember," the men said, "the oath you made us swear to will not be binding on us unless, when we enter the land, you have tied the scarlet cord from your window" (Joshua 2:17-18a, author's paraphrase). They also instructed her to keep all of her family inside the house, otherwise they would be killed.

The day finally arrived. Joshua began by conducting psychological warfare. He chose seven priests with trumpets and instructed them to walk in front of the ark. The armed guard marched ahead of the priests, and the rear guard followed the ark.

All the other Israelites walked behind. During this entire march, the trumpets were sounding, but the people were very quiet. For six days, they marched around the city and then returned to Gilgal. On the seventh day, they left at daybreak before most of the people of Jericho were awake. They did exactly what they had done before, except that they marched around the city seven times. On the seventh march, when the trumpets sounded, Joshua gave the signal and the hordes of Israelites shouted at once. With that, all the walls of the city "came tumbling down." Joshua declared that all in the city should be destroyed except for Rahab and those within her house (Joshua 6:8-25).

The beautiful end of the story is that Rahab became a believer. She married Salmon, one of the spies, and became a part of the lineage of Jesus, for their son was Boaz, who married Ruth (see Matthew 1:5).

This story reminds me that we serve a God and a Christ of second chances. We don't have to stay the way we are. We are Christians under construction. One of my favorite verses in the New Testament is this: "He who began a good work in you will carry it on to completion" (Philippians 1:6, NIV). I am counting on that!

What Can We Learn From Rahab?

Lesson 1: If you have faith in God, even "the size of a mustard seed" (Matthew 17:20), God can push wide the door of your heart, come to dwell therein, and transform your life.

Rahab had only heard stories of God's mighty works at the Red Sea. Many others had heard the same stories and doubted; but Rahab believed, and her life was forever different. I am convinced that God's prevenient grace—which goes before us to prepare the way—had surrounded her life, even as it had for Abraham and Sarah. All three knew nothing "personal" about this one true God, but they opened the doors of their hearts, and God used them in spectacular ways to further his plan of redemption.

There are many today who have little or no faith in the one true God, just as there were in Rahab's day; and there are many who do not believe in God's only Son, Jesus Christ. Yet when we encounter such individuals, we often don't bother even to engage them in an intelligent discussion about God or Christianity. Sometimes it is because we don't want to appear "fanatical," or we simply haven't organized our beliefs into an intelligent, winsome witness. All around us are people who are unbelievers, nominal Christians, and searchers who need answers to serious questions. As responsible Christians, we must be ready at a moment's notice to articulate our beliefs intelligently and with sensitivity. What's more, if our witness is to be effective, our words must be backed up by our Christian living—our everyday example. In other words, our deeds must square with our words. We also must genuinely care about the person we are seeking to reach.

Such an opportunity came to me this year. In our city, there is a boutique for women where I go occasionally to buy shoes or a purse. The store buyer is an attractive, very chic woman. One day I went into the store and thought that she looked somewhat troubled. When she finished with her customer, I walked over to her and asked, "Are you all right today?" She shook her head and motioned for me to follow her into a dressing room. Once inside, she told me the story. In a routine physical examination several weeks earlier, the doctor thought he saw "something suspicious" on an x-ray of her liver and suggested she have an MRI. They discovered she had a tumor that turned out to be malignant. Her oncologist wanted her to go to a renowned surgeon in another city to see what procedure he would suggest.

Her eyes told me that she was terrified. She is divorced and lives alone. Her only daughter lives out of the country; and although her son is in America, he lives in another city. He was coming to take her to see the surgeon. Sensing that she wanted something more from me, I asked, "Would you like for me to have a prayer with you?" Tears welled up in her eyes as she replied, "Would you, please?"

At that point I didn't know anything about her faith background. Later, I learned that she had grown up in a church, but that faith was not operative in her life. Before she was to leave town for her surgery, I stopped by to have another prayer with her. I promised that my husband and I would be on the "hotline" for her during the hours of her surgery. She seemed very appreciative. When she returned home, her daughter came to be with her. From time to time, I ran by with some food that I thought might be appealing to her as she recuperated from surgery.

Though we are from different countries, cultures, and churches (she is Catholic and I am Protestant), the two of us have become friends. Now, if I have an especially difficult schedule, she says with a smile, "I'll be on the 'hotline' for you." My purpose in extending kindness was not to recruit a member for my church, but to rekindle her faith in the One who "is able to accomplish abundantly far more than all we can ask or imagine" (Ephesians 3:20).

Obviously, God's prevenient grace had gone before to prepare her heart for my visit. I simply planted a seed, but it was God who provided the harvest. God was the one who caused the seed to grow into a beautiful flower of faith. In addition, I was given a warm friendship to bless my life.

Sometimes the faith of even the strongest Christian can waver, and God needs a human who is willing to be available to show God's love and remind the wavering Christian of God's constant presence. Katherine Von Bora, a former nun who became the wife of Martin Luther, was such a person. She encouraged her husband mightily during the tumultuous days of the Protestant

Reformation. According to Edith Deen, author of *Great Women of the Christian Faith* (Harper & Brothers Publishers, 1959), Katherine lived up to the Proverbs 31 ideal of wife and mother: "Her husband has full confidence in her / and lacks nothing of value" (Proverbs 31:11, NIV).

Even Martin Luther, a man of strong faith and Christian conviction, occasionally lost his usual cheerfulness and became moody. At such times, Katherine sought to comfort and encourage him. Her efforts were usually successful. There was one time, however, when nothing seemed to lift his spirits and he left home for a few days. When he returned, he found his wife seated in the middle of the room. She was dressed in black, had a black cloth thrown over her head, and looked quite sad. When he inquired what was wrong, she replied: "Only think, my dear doctor, the Lord in heaven is dead, and this is the cause of my grief." Laughing heartily, Luther said: "It is true, dear Kate; I am acting as if there was no God in heaven." Luther's melancholy left him immediately (*Great Women of the Christian Faith*, pp. 93–94).

At times I have encouraged others in their faith, and at other times I have been the one who was encouraged. I am so thankful for all the encouragers in my life who have come alongside me when I was weary and my faith was wavering. Isn't it reassuring to remember that our faith doesn't have to be strong all the time. All we really need is a seed. And if we hold onto that seed of faith, God can transform our lives.

Lesson 2: Our past does not have to determine our future.

Some people choose to live in the past. Instead of living fully in the present, they use their mental energy reliving happy or unhappy events, or dreading the future. But as Ecclesiastes 3:1 tells us, "For everything there is a season," and *today* is the season for living fully. As the psalmist reminds us, "This is the day that the LORD has made; / let us rejoice and be glad in it" (Psalm

118:24). In order to rejoice and be glad and live fully today—even as we "lean" toward the future—we must do three things.

First, we must "turn loose" the past. God said to Lot and his wife as they left the city of Sodom, "Do not look back" (Genesis 19:17), yet Lot's wife couldn't resist. Perhaps, as she was looking at that pagan place, she was thinking of the good times she had enjoyed there. She didn't want to be destroyed in the city, but she didn't want to leave either. Remember what happened to her? She turned into a pillar of salt. Once I told that story to some inner-city children, and a little boy raised his hand. He said, "My mama looked back to the back seat to see what we were doing, and she turned into a telephone pole." Well, we won't turn into a pillar of salt or a telephone pole by looking back, but we will never become instruments that are splendidly ready for God's using in the here and now.

Second, if our past is full of mistakes, bad decisions, or disobedience to God's laws, we must truly repent and receive God's forgiveness. Jesus told us, "Ask, and it will be given you; search, and you will find; knock, and the door will be opened for you" (Matthew 7:7). It's as simple as that: When we ask God to forgive our sins, we receive God's forgiveness. If we do not repent, however, we will be burdened by guilt that will hang on like barnacles on a ship; and just as barnacles prevent a ship from being seaworthy, our guilt will prevent us from being "life-worthy."

None of us *deserves* God's forgiveness; it is a gift freely given. This is why often we are unwilling to forgive ourselves. We realize the enormity of the wrong we have committed, and we continue to be consumed by guilt. But if God has forgiven us—and God has if we are truly sorry and ask for forgiveness—how do we dare not receive the gift?

Rahab evidently received that gift; what's more, she didn't "look back" or bemoan the fact that she no longer had her material possessions. She believed that the powerful God, of whom she had heard so much, would direct her life—and, indeed, God did. The opening lines of the New Testament tell us of the significant plan God had for her: "Salmon the father of Boaz [whose mother was Rahab], Boaz the father of Obed, whose mother was Ruth; Obed the father of Jesse, Jesse the father of King David…; [and] Jacob the father of Joseph, the husband of Mary of whom was born Jesus Who is called the Christ" (Matthew 1:5-6a, 16, AMP). God doesn't look at what we have been but looks at what we can become.

Some people refuse to follow God's example of forgiving and letting go; instead, they lock us into what we have been. Even some of the first disciples and early Christians were guilty of holding onto the past, for they would not believe that God had transformed Paul's life from persecutor of Christians to dynamic evangelist and missionary. Are you doing the same thing to anyone you know—including, perhaps, yourself?

Once we have let go of the past and accepted God's forgiveness, we are ready to do the third thing that enables us to live fully today as we lean toward the future.

Lesson 3: We must keep our eyes upon Jesus and stay focused on the task he is calling us to do.

In my Sunday school class, we often sing a chorus of "Turn Your Eyes Upon Jesus," a hymn that describes our need for Christ-centered living and turns our attention to the glory and grace of Christ. To focus on Jesus and the task he is calling us to do requires that we spend time with him, and the "bonus" is that the cares of this world fall into the proper perspective.

Do you ever have the feeling that your life is set on "fast forward"? Before the advent of television, life seemed slower and simpler. This is not just the sound of nostalgia speaking; the scientific community, including medical doctors and psychiatrists, tells us that the noise and distraction levels of our world today are increasing our stress at an alarming rate. Some households, I am told, never turn off the television set from the time they awaken until they go to bed at night. They have no idea of the wonder of silence.

As a young person, one of my favorite movies was *Gone with the Wind.* The Civil War seemed more real to me in that film than in any of my American history classes. I must have seen the movie at least seven times while I was growing up. Years later, when my husband noted that the original film was going to be seen on television, we made plans to watch it. Fortunately, the three-hour film had been edited for television viewing; but even so, the plot seemed to move like a tortoise, and the dialogue was agonizingly slow at times. *My goodness*, I thought, *What has happened to us? If someone doesn't speak in six-second sound bites, we become bored.* The danger is that we will live fast but not deeply, leaving no time for creative thought or prayerful listening. How can God get through to fragmented and distracted minds and hearts?

Recently my husband and I returned from a week at Lakeside, Ohio—the Chautauqua on Lake Erie—where I was speaker for the week. It was our fourth season there, and once again I came away calmer and more relaxed than when I arrived. Why? One reason is the beauty of the setting. Lakeside is located on the Marblehead peninsula, halfway between Toledo and Cleveland, and the sunsets over Lake Erie are worth the trip alone. For more than 125 years, thousands of persons have traveled across the country to enjoy one of America's few remaining Chautauqua-type communities. It is a place where you can get away from the static of the world and renew the body, mind, and spirit. From the moment you drive through the gates to this historic, Victorian community clustered around a large auditorium, time seems almost irrelevant. Everything moves more slowly, and everybody smiles more readily. Most people, from the oldest to the youngest—and there are tons of children and young people—ride bikes and walk; and most everybody stops by "The Patio" for the biggest ice cream cone in the country. Lakeside programs include worship, lectures, seminars, book reviews, symphonies, ballets, operas, outdoor recreation, and entertainment.

Just as people must choose to go to Lakeside (or "Shangri-La," as I have named it), so also we must choose places for quiet and rest and prayerful reading of God's Word each day. Only then can we think creatively and listen prayerfully as God seeks to communicate God's love and purposes to us. Despite her background and the fact that she knew little about him, god communicated his love and purposes to Rahab. Centuries ago the prophet Isaiah reminded us of our need for time alone with God when he wrote: "Those who wait for the LORD shall renew their strength, / they shall mount up with wings like eagles, / they shall run and not be weary, / they shall walk and not faint" (Isaiah 40:31). Likewise, Isaiah wrote: "In quietness and in confidence shall be your strength" (30:15c, KJV).

Our younger son was born in a wonderful Catholic hospital. The sister in charge of the hospital visited patients regularly. One day, as she "breezed in" for a visit, I asked, "Where do you get all that energy?" With a twinkle in her eye, she replied, "I get my gasoline from the Lord." So can we in periods of quiet and prayer.

Polish pianist and composer Ignacy Yan Paderewski is reported to have said, "If I don't practice for one day, I know it; if I don't practice for two days, the critics know it; if I don't practice for three days, the audience knows it." I feel much the same about a quiet time of prayer, Bible study, and listening. If I miss one day, I know it. Feeling fragmented and lethargic are the evidences, no matter how I try to conceal them. If I miss two days, my family knows it. They notice that I am harried and sometimes more easily irritated. If I miss three days, everyone with whom I come in contact knows that something is wrong. They notice that I lack energy and enthusiasm and that I am not as "present" to them as I should be.

William Wordsworth wrote these words:

> The world is too much with us, . . .
>> Getting and spending, we lay waste our powers:
>> Little we see in Nature that is ours.

His words are as relevant today as they were when he wrote them in 1806. We seem to be moving at dizzying speeds, and unless we have regular spaces of quiet, silence, and prayer, we will spin further and further away from the core of our being. It is in my daily quiet time of reading God's Word and then being still long enough to allow my spirit to catch up with my body that I receive some of "God's nudges." My quiet time renews my energy, enlivens my spirit, and makes me see my direction more clearly.

Lesson 4: Instead of being content to live in "the shallows," we must launch out into "the deep waters" of faith and do something courageous for God.

In order to be true to our Christian convictions, we sometimes must take a stand that may be dangerous—or, at least, unpopular. After his disciples had fished all night on the Sea of Galilee and had caught nothing, Jesus said, "Launch out into the deep, and let down your nets for a draught" (Luke 5:4, KJV). Today Jesus is saying the same thing to us regarding the waters of faith: "Launch out into the deep; don't live in the shallows."

For years, though I had learned the techniques of swimming, I was terrified of deep water. When our younger son graduated from the shallow end to the deep end of the pool, I knew that if there was to be any family togetherness in the pool, it would have to be in the deep end. So I took my pride in hand and joined an adult beginners class. The class consisted mainly of other women like me, all trying to keep up with our families.

I got along great in that class until the day the instructor said, "Today we are going to the deep end of the pool." I did something very "Christian": I let everybody go ahead of me! When the instructor said to the class, "Jump in," others jumped in as if they weren't afraid at all. Finally, only she and I were standing outside the pool. She said quietly but firmly, "Jump in." I looked down at that deep water, and everything in me rebelled. "I can't; I just can't do it," I said.

Then she asked me, "Do you believe that this water will hold you up?" Well, I knew that it was the same water that had held me up in the shallow end, and I could see that it was holding everybody else up. "Yes, I believe that it will," I replied meekly. "Then act like you do," she said. "Jump in." She was calling my bluff. She was saying, "You either believe it or you don't, and the test is at the point of action." There was nothing to do but jump; so I closed my eyes and thought of the good life I had had until then. I never really expected to come out of that water. Then I learned something that most people have known for years: It is actually easier to swim in deep water.

As I came out of the pool that day, I realized that there is a spiritual analogy in my swimming experience. Just as I had to learn to "trust" the water in order to swim in deep water, so also all of us must learn to trust the waters of faith—especially when there are storms and rough seas in our lives. Unfortunately, many people go to church for years and never get out of the "shallow water." Many people say, "I believe in God; in Jesus Christ, God's Son and my Savior; and in the Holy Spirit," yet they are not willing to venture beyond their "comfort zone" and discover what it really means to be a disciple of Christ. The test is at the point of action. Either we sincerely believe, or we don't; either we follow the teachings and example of Christ, or we don't; either we serve others in his name, or we don't. And if we *do*, then we cannot avoid "the deep waters" of faith.

Rahab certainly launched out into "the deep waters" of faith—faith in a God she hardly knew. She trusted, and God fulfilled God's promises. The beautiful result was that she is in the lineage of Jesus Christ, our Savior and Lord.

Digging a Little Deeper

1. Read Joshua 2:1-24. How do you account for the faith of Rahab, who never knew anyone who believed in the one true God until she hid the Israelite spies on her rooftop?
2. Read Matthew 17:20. What did Jesus mean when he said that God can do mighty acts through us if we have faith no larger than a mustard seed?
3. Do people who know you want to know more about the God you serve? How do you know? Are you able to share your faith intelligently and winsomely? Why or why not? If not, where can you turn for help? With whom have you shared your faith recently—whether directly or indirectly? What happened?
4. Do you believe that we don't have to stay the way we are—that our past does not have to determine our future? Why or why not? What did Jesus teach us about this? See 2 Corinthians 5:17 and Philippians 1:6.
5. How do we know that Rahab didn't stay the way she was before the Israelite spies came? Read Matthew 1:5.
6. Is there anything in your past that needs to be forgiven so that you can move on with your life? Do you need to ask to be forgiven by God and/or by someone else? What can you do to bring about reconciliation and/or restoration?
7. Do you believe that our stress levels are higher today than those of persons in years past because we are living faster but not as deeply? Is this partly due to noise levels and the number of distractions we encounter? Why do you think this?

8. Do you believe that staying focused on Jesus can anchor us more securely? Read and respond to Matthew 14:22-33.

9. What Bible affirmations help you grow calmer and more peaceful? Use a Bible concordance to find verses including the words *peace* and *rest*. (Also see "Affirmations for the Journey Ahead," below)

10. Read Luke 5:4-9. Jesus told his disciples to "launch out into the deep" to catch more fish (verse 4, KJV). How do these same words apply to us in "spiritual waters"?

11. What keeps you from "launching out into the deep" in areas where you feel God is calling you? What can you do about it?

Affirmations for the Journey Ahead

Use the following affirmations whenever you are tired, harried, stressed, anxious, or worried—or, in other words, any time you need the peace of God, "which surpasses all understanding" (Philippians 4:7). They are especially effective to use at the beginning of your quiet time.

"Be still, and know that I am God!" (Psalm 46:10).

"Thou wilt keep him in perfect peace, whose mind is stayed on thee" (Isaiah 26:3, KJV).

"Come to me, all you who are weary and burdened, and I will give you rest" (Matthew 11:28, NIV).

"My peace I give unto you: not as the world giveth, give I unto you. Let not your heart be troubled, neither let it be afraid" (John 14:27, KJV).

8.

Courage to Take a Risk

Scripture Text: **The Book of Esther (Chapters 1–10)**

"Who knows but that you have come to royal position for such a time as this?"

—Esther 4:14, NIV

"Go, gather together all the Jews who are in Susa, and fast for me. Do not eat or drink for three days, night or day. I and my maids will fast as you do. When this is done, I will go to the king, even though it is against the law. And if I perish, I perish."

—Esther 4:16, NIV

Esther's Story

If possible, read the ten short chapters of the Book of Esther before reading my story of this beautiful Persian queen. You will be able to tell immediately the few places where I have "filled in" with my imagination.

Esther was preparing the evening meal for her beloved cousin Mordecai, who had adopted her when her father and mother had died. From the time she was a small child, he had been the only "parent" she had known. Suddenly, Mordecai burst into the house, coming home from his job as a palace guard at the king's gate.

Breathlessly he said, "Quick, Esther, choose your prettiest dress and put it on. I am going to take you down to be considered as one of the contestants for the new queen."

"The new queen?" asked Esther in total surprise. "What happened to Queen Vashti?"

"Didn't I tell you what happened?" said Mordecai.

When she shook her head from side to side, Mordecai told how King Xerxes (or King Ahasuerus, as he is called in some translations) had gathered together all the leading men of the empire to the capital city of Susa. It was a huge affair, lasting 180 days, or six months (Esther 1:3-4). Xerxes displayed the vast wealth of the kingdom and the glory of his majesty. When these days were drawing to an end, the king held a banquet that lasted seven days. It was held in the enclosed garden of the palace. He not only invited leading men in the empire, but he also included all the men from the least to the greatest in the capital city. At the banquet, there were couches of gold and silver on a mosaic of porphyry—marble, mother of pearl, and other costly stones. Wine was served in gold goblets, each one different from the others, and the King commanded each guest to drink as much wine as he liked.

"Oh, yes, I have heard about the extravagant banquet," said Esther, somewhat impatiently. "But what happened to Queen Vashti?"

"Well," said Mordecai, "on the last night of the banquet, when most of the men had drunk too much wine, especially the king, he sent for the Queen, telling her to put on her royal robes and her crown and come into the banquet hall to display her beauty. But she refused to go."

"Good for her," said Esther. "I certainly would not want to parade around in front of hundreds of drunken men."

"Unfortunately, it wasn't good for Vashti," said Mordecai. "The king was furious, and he consulted his chief counselors. They advised him to take drastic action against the queen. Otherwise, her example would encourage other wives to disobey their husbands. The king, they said, should issue a decree banning Vashti from his presence and confer her position on a worthier woman."

"But where will she go, and how will she live?" asked the astonished Esther.

"No one knows," said Mordecai. "But an edict has gone out for a search of all the beautiful virgins in the empire. The chief eunuch, Hegai, will select the most beautiful ones, and those chosen will receive special beauty treatments, six months with oil of myrrh, and six months with perfumes and cosmetics. And Hadassah [that was Esther's Hebrew name, though she was known by her Persian name], no woman is more beautiful than you, so I want to take you to Hegai."

"Oh, cousin Mordecai, you have always seen me through the eyes of love, and I thank you for that. But you know as well as I that a Jewish girl would not be chosen as queen of Persia, the most glorious of today's empires."

"There is no need to reveal your ancestry," said the respected Mordecai. "I want to present you to the chief eunuch."

"I have never disobeyed you, cousin Mordecai, and I won't start now," Esther replied meekly.

When she was taken to meet Hegai, it was obvious that Esther's beauty pleased the eunuch. In fact, because of her kindness and humility as well as her beauty, Esther found favor with everyone. Hegai gave her seven maids to attend her and moved all of them to the best place in the harem. In addition, she was presented to the king in the tenth month. He was attracted to her more than he was to any of the other virgins (Esther 2:17). So it was that King Xerxes had a banquet for all the nobles and officials, at which time he placed a royal crown on Esther's head and proclaimed her queen of Persia (Esther 2:17-18).

Soon after Esther had moved into the palace, Mordecai overheard two of the palace guards planning to assassinate the king. He sent the message to Esther, who in turn told the king. After confirming the report, the king had both of the guards killed.

Now there was man in the empire whose name was Haman. He was liked by the king and was named chief minister. Already a man with a strong ego, Haman's new appointment only increased his egotism. Haman soon asked for an edict that would have everyone in the empire bow down as he, Haman, walked past them. Xerxes, a generous but detached king, agreed. All the people in the palace area, except Mordecai, obeyed the edict. As a strong follower of God, Mordecai believed that you should bow to no one except the one true God. When Haman heard this, he was furious—not only with Mordecai but also with all the Jews who lived in Persia. When Haman found the king in a good mood, he cleverly presented his argument: "There is a certain people dispersed and scattered among the peoples in all the provinces of your kingdom whose customs are different from those of all other people and who do not obey the king's laws; it is not in the king's best interest to tolerate them. If it pleases the king, let a decree be issued to destroy them, and I will put ten thousand talents of silver into the royal treasury for the men who carry out this business" (Esther 3:8-9, NIV).

The king told him to keep his money and to do with the people what he would. Of course, the king had no idea that his queen was one of the people Haman's decree would destroy. The edict was issued. When Mordecai read it, he put on sackcloth and ashes and went out into the city wailing bitterly and loudly. He went as far as the king's gate, for no one wearing sackcloth and ashes could go beyond the gate (Esther 4:1-2).

When Esther's maids brought her word of Mordecai's behavior, she was distressed and sent him clothes to put on. He refused. Then she sent the eunuch assigned to her to determine what was troubling Mordecai. He told the eunuch exactly what had happened and sent a copy of the edict to Esther, urging her to go before the king and plead for her people.

Her message back to him was that everyone knew you didn't just go into the king's presence without being bidden. If you did, you would die. There was one exception. If King Xerxes lifted the golden scepter, he dissolved the rule; but apparently that didn't happen often. She added that he had not called her for thirty days.

Mordecai's response was immediate and firm. He told her not to think that because she was in the king's house, she alone would escape. If she remained silent, he said, relief for the Jews would come from another source; but she and her father's family would surely perish. Then he added the words that have echoed through the centuries. Certainly they have been the subject of many sermons and the impetus of much soul-searching on the part of individuals: "Who knows but that you have come to royal position for such a time as this?" (Esther 4:14, NIV).

Esther must have struggled with her decision, but in this crisis, she put all thought of herself aside. Then she sent this reply to Mordecai: "Go, gather together all the Jews who are in Susa, and fast for me. Do not eat or drink for three days, night or day. I and my maids will fast as you do. When this is done, I will go to the king, even though it is against the law. And if I perish, I perish" (Esther 4:16, NIV). What courage that must have taken!

Evidently, during the days of fasting and prayer, Esther was given a plan of action to use in the event that the king would see her. She must have looked beautiful, regal, and desirable in her royal gowns as she walked into the throne room. The king must have been pleased when he saw her because he held out the golden scepter, which meant she could approach. Obviously in a good mood, the king asked what her request was, adding these words: "Even up to half the kingdom, it will be given you" (5:3).

"If it pleases the king," replied Esther, "let the king, together with Haman, come today to a banquet I have prepared for him" (Esther 5:4). The king sent for Haman, and they attended the queen's banquet. Again the king wanted to know her request, offering her half of his kingdom. Again, she invited the king and Haman to a banquet the following evening. No one knows whether she lost her nerve to say what she had planned to say. I believe that she was flattering Haman so that he would trip himself up, which indeed he did.

On the way home that evening, Haman was feeling great about being invited twice with the king to the queen's banquet. Later that evening he told his wife and friends how wealthy he was and what favor he had found with the king. Yet he said that all this gave him no satisfaction as long as he saw that Jew, Mordecai, sitting at the king's gate, refusing to bow down when he passed by. They suggested that he build a seventy-five–foot gallows and get the king's permission to have Mordecai hung on it. Then he could attend the queen's banquet and have nothing to mar the occasion. The idea appealed to the egotistical Haman.

God was at work in the process, however, because that night the king was sleepless and decided to read. He ordered that the court records be brought to him. Soon he saw the entry about Mordecai's having revealed the plot to assassinate the king. "What was done to reward Mordecai?" he asked the courtiers. "Nothing has been done," they replied (Esther 6:1-4).

About that time there was a noise in the outer court. "Who's there?" asked the king. It was Haman, who couldn't wait to receive approval for Mordecai to be hung on the gallows. But before Haman could speak, the king asked, "What should be done for the man the king delights to honor?" (Esther 6:6, NIV). Thinking that he was the man the king was referring to, Haman strutted around the room, suggesting that the man should be dressed in one of the king's royal robes and placed on one of the king's horses—one that had the royal crest on its head. Then the man and the horse should be led through the streets of the city by one of the king's noble princes, who would say, "This is what is done for the man the king delights to honor" (Esther 6:9, NIV). The king liked the idea and sent Haman to do just that for Mordecai! Can you imagine Haman's mortification?

At the second banquet, when the king asked for Esther's request, she replied, "If it pleases your majesty, then may my life be granted at my petition and my people at my request?" (Esther 7:3, author's paraphrase).

A bewildered king asked what she meant. Then she admitted her Jewish blood for the first time, and she explained that the Jews had been sold to be destroyed, killed, and obliterated. In indignation, the king asked who had dared contemplate such a thing. When Esther told him it was Haman, the king was furious.

Haman cowered in terror at the king's fury; and when the king strode out into the garden to quiet his rage, Haman flung himself onto the couch where the queen was reclining to beg for his life. At that moment, the king stalked into the room, and seeing Haman on the couch, cried out: "Will he even molest the queen while she is with me in the house?" (Esther 7:8, NIV). The king ordered the attendants to seize Haman and have him hung on the very gallows Haman had constructed for Mordecai.

Though the edict concerning the Jews could not be rescinded (it was a part of the law of the Medes and Persians), Xerxes issued another edict that allowed the Jews in every city to carry arms and to protect themselves against anyone who sought to hurt them. This incident instituted a new Jewish feast—the Feast of Purim, which is a day of joy and feasting, a day for giving presents to one another (Esther 9:19). The Feast of Purim continues to be celebrated until this day.

What Can We Learn From Esther?

Lesson 1: In a time of crisis, we must have courage.

To those of us living under Western democracy, the act of a queen approaching a king may seem insignificant—certainly not an act requiring courage. But in the Middle Eastern culture, where ruling kings have absolute power, the possibility of assassination was very real. Hence the law that no one could approach the king without being invited seemed reasonable.

Esther, the orphan Jewish girl and one of generations of Jews forced to live in captivity, naturally would be hesitant to approach the ruler of her country. In addition, she had been queen for only a very short time, and she didn't want to die. It was her faith—and the three days of prayer and fasting held by her and her fellow believers—that imbued her spirit with wisdom and courage. In the crisis, she was able to rise above all thoughts of herself and seek the common good.

As I reread the story of this brave Jewish woman, I thought of Corrie ten Boom, a brave Christian woman from the Netherlands who, because of her faith, risked her life to help many Jews escape Hitler's death edict for the Jews during World War II. Because they believed that this was wrong, she and her family in Haarlem, Holland, hid Jewish families above her father's watch shop. Eventually they were arrested, and Corrie and her younger sister, Betsie, were sent to Ravensbrook Concentration Camp. Betsie died there because of the horrible conditions in the camp. Corrie was released unexpectedly in 1945, and she began immediately to establish rehabilitation homes in Holland for concentration camp victims, as well as homes for refugees in Germany. Through her writing and speaking, she told the story of her experiences and bore witness to her faith in Jesus Christ. It was Christ, she said, who gave her the courage to help her Jewish neighbors and who encouraged her in her imprisonment. Three of her books—*The Hiding Place, Tramp for the Lord,* and *In My Father's House*—have not only increased my own faith but also have imbued me with courage.

Today, we must live out our faith in a secular culture with a great diversity of faiths. Although I believe we must be respectful of the faiths of others, it is important that we know what we believe as Christians and have the courage to present our faith in an intelligent and winsome way. Even more courage will be required to stand against secular practices that are destructive— especially for our children and youth. But, as representatives of Christ, we must do it!

Lesson 2: In a time of crisis, we must be clever.

Esther was clever as well as courageous. She used her head, even though her heart was heavy with fear for her own life as well as for the lives of her people. In her time of prayer, she obviously was given a plan. Then she planned carefully before she approached the king.

Jesus warned us about what we are likely to be up against in the world when he said, "See, I am sending you out like sheep into the midst of wolves; so be wise as serpents and innocent as doves" (Matthew 10:16). It seems to me that Esther did both. She was aware of who she was up against—Haman, a ruthless, deceitful, egotistical opportunist. Yet she didn't run to the king, whining, crying, and accusing Haman behind his back. Instead, she staged the banquet in her own setting. The invitation to her two banquets inflated Haman's ego so that he was totally unprepared for the factual accusation she gave the king in Haman's presence. Esther gave Haman enough rope to hang himself easily, and he did.

Where did Esther get her cleverness—her control and wisdom? I believe the three days of prayer prepared her. James tells us: "If any of you is lacking in wisdom, ask God, who gives to all generously and ungrudgingly, and it will be given you" (1:5). Unlike Esther, we often charge into a situation without having our emotions in control, without having thought clearly or asked God for wisdom—especially when a crisis takes us by surprise. But if we will take time to call upon God, he will give us the wisdom we need.

As I have prepared this chapter on Esther, the well-known poem "If" by Rudyard Kipling has come to mind often. The last line is my own paraphrase:

> If you can keep your head when all about you
>   Are losing theirs and blaming it on you,
> . . . .
> If you can dream—and not make dreams your master;
>   If you can think—and not make thoughts your aim;
> If you can meet with Triumph and Disaster
>   And treat those two impostors just the same;
> . . . .
> If you can talk with crowds and keep your virtue,
>   Or walk with Kings—nor lose the common touch,
> If neither foes nor loving friends can hurt you,
>   If all men count with you, but none too much;
> Yours is the Earth and everything that's in it,
> And—what is more—you will be a person of God, my
>   child!

Life is a balancing act. In Matthew 10:16, I believe that Jesus was saying that we must be wise, not naive, in the ways of the world. Only then will our voices be heard. Yet we must stand firm on our Christian convictions so that we can be as innocent as doves. This is what it means to be in the world but not "of the world" (John 15:19, KJV). Like Esther, we must be wise and yet innocent.

Lesson 3: God can take a "Cinderella" and turn her into a princess.

God can take us, with all our mistakes and idiosyncrasies, and, if we are willing and faithful, turn us into persons of peace, poise, and power.

The story of Esther is a true Cinderella story. Esther was an orphan. We don't know whether her parents were somehow killed or died of natural causes. We don't know if they died at the same time or several years apart. We know only that Mordecai took his uncle's daughter, Esther, and reared her as his own. Like Cinderella, Esther was "lovely in form and features" (Esther 2:7, NIV). And like Cinderella, Esther was underprivileged. In Cinderella's case, the cause was poverty; for Esther, it was her inclusion in a minority group. Her forebears had lived in Jerusalem and were taken into captivity when King Nebuchadnezzar was king of Babylon. Through the years, a number of families had returned to Jerusalem, but many remained in Persia where they had found a livelihood. Esther's family was one of the latter. Like Cinderella, Esther had not only physical beauty but also a good mind, kindness, and humility (or a teachable spirit). That combination is what I call "charm." There is nothing phony or pretentious about real charm. For most people, charm is an indefinable quality—"you know it when you see it." *The New World Dictionary* defines charm as "a quality or feature in someone or something that attracts and delights people." I like the definition of charm in the play *What Every Woman Knows*, by Sir James M. Barrie: "Charm is a kind of bloom on a woman. If she has it, she doesn't need anything else. If she doesn't have it, it doesn't much matter what else she has." Esther definitely had it.

Yet with all her beauty and charm, Esther never could have been so courageous and wise and influential in her own strength. It was the power of God at work in her life. Because she had a strong faith, she sought God's direction and was willing to be used for God's purposes (Esther 4:16). Her life and the life of her people were forever different.

God is at work in our lives, though we often see it best in retrospect. Remember that God's time is not marked by our calendars. Our job is to take time to listen carefully to God's direction, to be steadfast in our responsibilities, and to trust God for the future.

Sometimes when I think I can't possibly do what must be done, I think of Susanna Wesley (1669–1742), the mother of nineteen children, including John Wesley, founder of the Methodist movement, and Charles Wesley, evangelist and song writer. Susanna not only home-schooled her children, but she also spent an hour weekly with each of them for Bible study and Christian instruction. In addition, she was a minister's wife; and in that day, there were specific responsibilities connected with the role. Since her husband was not a good financial manager, she often had to shoulder responsibility for the care of the farm they established to help sustain their family. In her biography *Susanna Wesley, The Mother of Methodism* (London: The Epworth Press, 1938; p. 53), Mabel Brailsford answered some of my questions when she wrote: "When we ask ourselves how twenty-four hours could hold all normal activities, which she, a frail young woman of thirty, was able to crowd into them, the answer may be found in [the] two hours of daily retirement when she drew from God, in the quietness of her own room, peace and patience, and an indefatigable courage."

When we turn to God, as Susanna Wesley did, we, too, are able to meet our responsibilities with peace, patience, and indefatigable courage.

Digging a Little Deeper

1. Read Esther 4:9-11, 16. Why did it require courage for Esther to approach her husband with the request regarding her people? What gave her the courage to approach the king?

2. Read Esther 5:4-8. Did Esther have a thoughtful plan for approaching the king? How do you know?

3. Read Esther 5:1-2. What did the king do to show Esther that she could approach the throne?

4. Read Esther 5:4-8; 7:1-10. What evidence do these verses give to prove that Esther was clever as well as courageous?

5. Read Matthew 10:16. What characteristics must we have as we approach evil people and situations? How did Esther exhibit these qualities?

6. Reread Rudyard Kipling's poem "If" on page 124. Which lines do you think best describe Esther? Why?

7. In what ways was Esther like Cinderella? How was she different?

8. How do you see God at work in this story? (See Esther 2:7-9; 5:1-2; 6:1-3; 8:11-12.)

9. Consider your own life and tell some of the ways you have seen God at work. What is your responsibility if God is to be more operative in your life?